# A  GREAT  RICH  MAN

*The Romance of Sir Walter Scott*

**LONGMANS, GREEN AND CO.**
55 FIFTH AVENUE, NEW YORK
221 EAST 20TH STREET, CHICAGO
TREMONT TEMPLE, BOSTON
128 UNIVERSITY AVENUE, TORONTO


**LONGMANS, GREEN AND CO. Ltd.**
39 PATERNOSTER ROW, E C 4, LONDON
53 NICOL ROAD, BOMBAY
6 OLD COURT HOUSE STREET, CALCUTTA
167 MOUNT ROAD, MADRAS

**SIR WALTER SCOTT**

*From a painting by Sir Edwin Landseer*

# A GREAT RICH MAN
*The Romance of Sir Walter Scott*

BY

LOUISE SCHUTZ BOAS

LONGMANS, GREEN AND CO.
LONDON · NEW YORK · TORONTO
1929

BOAS

A GREAT RICH MAN


COPYRIGHT · 1929
BY LOUISE SCHUTZ BOAS


FIRST EDITION

*To*
*Ralph and Marie*

This is the story of a man who found literature magnificently profitable. To him poetry and prose were alike romantic in the sense that Big Business is romantic. More idyllic than the adventures of the heroes of his poems and novels were his own adventures through life, adventures in success measured in material things, in things purchasable by the hard round gold his pen earned for him. He was a poet whose feet were firm upon the earth; his were no starry visions. The trail he blazed was the broad highway of commercial success.

He was a lawyer whose days in the courtroom taught him the price of failure, the value of success. Prosperity was his goal. The romance of courtly adventure he lived imaginatively; the romance of piling up at one and the same time enormous wealth and immeasurable fame was his real life.

His own generation called him Greatest. Wordsworth, Coleridge, Shelley, Keats, and the youthful Browning sang; their genius brought neither large fame nor plentiful profits. *Pride and Prejudice* brought Jane Austen the merest modicum of praise and pennies. The effortless poems and novels of Scott brought such fortune as only the most modern of decades has been able to produce as the reward of writing, and such fame as has not yet been equalled. The world made a path to his hospitable door.

He fulfilled his wife's prophecy for him; he made himself *a great rich man.*

# LIST OF ILLUSTRATIONS

# CHAPTER I

*No sounder piece of British manhood was put together in that eighteenth century of time.*      —CARLYLE.

# A GREAT RICH MAN
## *The Romance of Sir Walter Scott*

### CHAPTER I

**I**

ONE SUNDAY in spring in the latter half of the eighteenth century a tall young man limped down the church steps. He had paused to talk to the sexton, and the congregation had dispersed. A sudden gust of rain overtook him midway down the stairs; adjusting his umbrella he went on, to collide violently with a young lady who had suddenly dashed out from her refuge in the portico.

The lame Hercules righted the umbrella, profusely apologizing. The young lady gathered her skirts and with a slight bow was off.

"But I say, you have no umbrella!" cried Hercules. "Will you no take mine?"

The young lady paused. After all it was raining very hard, and she had on her new cloak. And it wasn't as if she didn't know who he was; he probably hadn't ever noticed her, but who could help noticing him? They were neighbors, though he wasn't aware of it; and their mothers had been at school together. She had often

watched him go galloping by; she had often heard him
come home late at night singing old ballads. He didn't
shout those horrid tavern songs, not even when his voice
sounded thick with drink. She knew, because she was
often awake in the night, and her room faced the street.
It was too bad he was lame. He was so handsome.

He was standing towering over her, proffering his
umbrella. Before she lowered her own dark eyes she
had seen that his were grey and fringed with long silky
brown lashes, though his eyebrows were flaxen. After
all their way was the same; why shouldn't she walk
with him. . .

"I . . . I," she stammered. "You don't know me but
my mother knows your mother. We're neighbors. I'm
Williamina Stuart. . ."

Walter Scott came home for dinner in boisterously
good spirits. "Why haven't we known the Stuarts ?" he
asked his mother.

"The Stuarts ? why we do know them. Lady Jane
and I were schoolmates. I see her now and then."

"Well, I don't know them. I just met Miss Stuart by
accident — she was caught in the rain. Couldn't you
call on her mother ?"

It was not long before Walter could take his place in
the Stuarts' Edinburgh drawingroom, to chatter nonsense with the young people who flocked round young
Williamina, prominent among the youths who paid her
court. They talked literature and life, gathered about
her harp to sing choruses and rounds, admired her paintings, tried out their French, discussed the latest poems,

planned picnics and parties. Walter, being lame, could not dance but young ladies flattered him by their willingness to sit out with him, preferring his conversation to the thrill of dancing with less attractive young men. He would tell these Scotch lassies the stirring deeds and daring loves of the lairds from whom they all claimed descent. His mind was crammed with ballads, anecdotes, dramatic incidents, all which he recited not in the dry manner of their fathers, but like the veriest play-actor. Poetry on his lips was something more than rhymed words; it was music, action, fire, love. So great was his admiration for anything Scotch, so deep his veneration for his ancestors, so wide his acquaintance with legend, that he seemed the very embodiment of Scotland. Love of country and love of romance united to vivify his words. He seemed the very hero he was describing. Certainly of all Willie's admirers none could talk more entertainingly, none sing a gayer song, none add more merriment to a gathering. He was tall, handsome, vivacious; his ready laugh exhibited perfect teeth; his firm shapely hands were quick to rescue my lady's fan or adjust her scarf.

He cultivated popularity the more that he might shine in Willie's eyes. For with all his boyish ardor he was soon devoted to Williamina. She was a true beauty according to the current standards. Her dark brown curls fell over pale cheeks that were rosy enough when quick blushes came. Her dark hazel eyes were demurely downcast, displaying the length and thickness of her lashes. She cultivated a mild pensive expression which, however, gave way to the high spirits of youth. None was readier for a frolic. She could match Scott's boisterous humor with what might have seemed hoydenishness had she not been so very well born. Her parents were no dragons. Properly chaperoned she might romp as she would. She was the centre of a lighthearted group of whom Walter Scott was soon the leader.

His devotion did not pass unnoticed. When a slovenly youth discards his worn corduroy breeches and takes to spruce new clothes, when he slicks his hair and adjusts his neckcloth before the mirror, his altered appearance shouts his love. His brothers and his friends were soon bantering him, and finally his father took heed of the matter. The lad who had sometimes seemed to him too harebrained to give promise of amounting to anything creditable, who had dashed off on wild walks and rides when he was not bent double over a romance, who ever had a dozen schemes on hand to prevent his application to his studies, was now savagely reading law. All the solemn exhortations of a steady father, himself the most reputable of attorneys, had failed to stimulate him beyond a mastery of the technical side of the business of attorney and a negligent attendance upon the legal lectures of the University of Edinburgh. The smiles of one girl had set him off upon commendable application to the pursuit of a lawyer's gown.

The elder Scott belonged to the lesser branch of law; his was the office of an attorney; his son, however, should wear the gown and plead cases at court. The lad's new interest in his studies would soon bring him to the desired

WALTER SCOTT
FATHER OF THE NOVELIST
*From a painting at Abbotsford*

MRS. SCOTT
MOTHER OF THE NOVELIST

end of admittance to the bar. He would, however, for the most part have to make his own way; his father's office could assure him of a proper practice, could throw business his way, but he would have no large income settled upon him. As a lawyer of small means he was no match for the daughter of Sir John Stuart.

"My dear sir," the elder Walter Scott began, nodding toward the young people at the other end of the drawing-room, "has it come to your attention that my son is here very frequently ?"

"A fine young man," countered the lady's father. "You'll be making a fine lawyer out of him. The ladies are over fond o' him, I'm thinking."

"Ay, he's a good lad. And he might as well have his fun while he's young. But I'm fearing he's lost his heart to your daughter, sir."

"Nay, I think not. They're mair like brother and sister. It's books they're forever talking, not love, my dear sir."

"But 'tis Willie, Willie, Willie with him all day long. He scarce can speak of anything else. He has but to glimpse her scarlet bonnet through the window and he's up and away, his dinner clean forgot. It's no that I'd be minding; but I know, sir, that your daughter has prospects my son canna meet. 'Tis a grand match you'll be wanting for Willie."

"Ay. But we'll hope she's in no hurry to leave us yet. She's but seventeen. Let her play awhile, and then we'll see."

Having warned Sir John, Mr. Scott felt that his duty was done. He himself had no objections to Walter's attachment, especially as it seemed to have stirred his ambition. He merely did not want his rich neighbor to believe him a fortune hunter for his son.

The intimacy of the two young people ripened. Walter, resplendent now in white breeches, gay waistcoats, and coats of fashionable cut, danced attendance at musicales, teas, and parties. When Williamina went off to her father's country estate she was permitted to correspond with Walter. Of course her letters, before they were sealed and sent, were submitted to her mother's perusal. In those days young ladies were circumspect. They were taught no lady would write to a man anything that would bring to her cheek the slightest blush—and ladies blushed easily—if the recipient were unmannerly enough to show the letter to his cronies. So Walter and his Willie wrote each other fine long descriptions of scenery, amusing anecdotes of visitors and parties, romantic tales of their ancestors, and wise discussions of the literature that solaced their lonely hours. Walter transcribed for Willie the more interesting of the ballads he gathered in his tramps and rides about remote hamlets. There were, too, in these letters warm protestations of friendship, but Walter was too shy and the lady too coy for any term more ardent than friendship.

It was no secret among the friends of Scott that he was head over ears in love. He sighed, wrote sonnets to his lady's eyebrow (which he showed in confidence to his fellow lawyers), dreamt of success and preferment in his profession, paced up and down before his lady's window in the moonlight, pressed her hand fondly at meet-

ing and parting, arranged her scarf, turned the pages of
her music, was saddened beyond measure did she frown,
and fairly shouted for joy at her smile.   He was, in short,
nineteen, and in love for the first time.

He talked much at home and abroad of deathless
passion, of an eternity of true love, of the purity of
women, of the necessity for great deeds.   He had been
brought up to reverence Woman.   He might share an
occasional naughty tale with other young blades, but
their dissipations he did not share.   His father had been
a man of rigid morality; he had successfully implanted
in his son the same fastidiousness, the same respect for
women.   So Walter worshipped and hoped, worshipped
and despaired, worshipped and hoped.   He took comfort in the fact that Williamina preferred none of her
swains markedly unless it were himself.   She called him
her lame giant.   He did not resent her pity for his handicap, for any emotion from her was welcome, and then
her pity was secondary to her admiration for his strength,
his fine figure, his good spirits, his wit.

For three years they played together the one game that
never grows dull, he pursuing, she leading him on, shyly,
gently, irresistibly.   Other swains grew tired, deserted
to serve at other altars, Walter Scott stayed on at her side,
his incense ever burning.   Of course one didn't think
seriously of a young lawyer who had a long way to go
to earn enough for a fashionable lady's pocket money.
Williamina was a well-brought-up maiden.   She knew
that hearts were not to be given away for the asking;
young men might love, might woo, might adore, might

supplicate; young ladies were not to listen until they were sure that here at last was the right young man. And how did one know that he was the right young man? Why first of all, of course, one was told so by one's parents; and then one's heart would say so. But the heart did not speak first. If it did, one might fall into the predicament of loving a man who didn't fall in love in return. No; young men pled, young ladies fled.

Still it was fun to be pursued. It was not unpleasant to feel a youth's eyes following wherever one turned. Besides people were saying that Walter Scott was very talented. He might make his mark in the world. Meanwhile he was just a pleasant boy whom one liked to have about, just a neighbor. Anyhow he was just a boy. He was, in fact, two years older than she, but that made him infinitely younger; girls were so much more sensible.

She grew so used to his adoration that she became less circumspect. Her letters when she was away, her speech when she was near at hand, were less guarded. He saw with delight that she flushed when he came into the room. She was ever ready to accept his invitations to sit out a dance, to take a decorous stroll, to accompany his singing on her harp. She chattered French with him, borrowed his books, let him teach her Italian. She listened to his romancing and his poems. His plans for a magnificent career she applauded. He would go away from her his head hitting the stars; and next day would work so savagely at his law that his father would smile wisely.

The months slid happily by. Scott by no means neglected his young men friends; they walked, rode, and
sang together; went to the theatre and got mixed up in
a grand riot, had literary meetings and drinking bouts.
To his intimates he was constantly talking about his
love, his fears, and his hopes. He had now served at
his lady's altar nearly five years; he had hopes of publishing some verses soon, his income though still small
was steadily growing, he had chances of preferment.

By lucky chance his antiquarian interests were actually
fanned by his legal duties. He had early been appointed
one of the curators of the Advocates' Library which had
a rich store of old manuscripts: ancient deeds, records of
lands and families, topographical and genealogical treas-
ure trove which to Walter Scott spelt romance. The
young lawyer had plenty of time on his hands; he could
delve and burrow into the musty papers, feeding his
already swollen ancestor worship with new-found tales
of daring deeds. His nimbly dramatic mind vivified the
history he uncovered — real or legendary, it flowed from
his tongue with the animation that fascinated young
ladies. Walter Scott, the ladies felt, had much more to
say than the average young man who could talk only
of himself or his horses or his petty triumphs. Walter
Scott treated young ladies as if they had something in
their pretty heads, as if they could follow a discussion
of historical or literary significance. There was a subtle
flattery in his naïve assumption that they were interested
in these matters.

And then his attention was caught by the German

Bürger's ghostly ballad *Lenore*. Fascinated by the tale he ventured to translate it into verse, facile verses that tripped easily from his pen though in them the spectres rode more vigorously than one might expect of disembodied spirits. Here was something, however, to lay at his lady's feet. Surely Williamina would be pleased to have him come forward as a poet, even in translation. Elated he read his verses to all those who would lend a listening ear; readily he yielded to the suggestion that he have a few copies printed, one brilliantly bound and gilded as a worthy present to his love. So much was she pleased and flattered, so sincere sounded the praises of her friends that he began to plan a small quarto of translations.

Meanwhile his friends advised that he put his fortune to the test; he might well now find out how he stood with Williamina. If he felt that he dared not risk an absolute refusal he need not commit himself to a proposal; he could sound out the lady by discussing his prospects with her. Accordingly with much searching of soul and dictionaries he wrote his Willie the sort of letter young men have always written; he could not ask her to share his fortune *now;* but if his fortune should improve, if he could rise to the point where he had enough to offer her, would she, could she accept ?

Her answer was long in coming. He ran through a whole cycle of fears and hopes before he finally read her circumspect reply. She was much flattered; she appreciated his regard highly; she was as fond of him as if he were her brother; she believed that he was slated for fame and fortune; she felt that he would really succeed. He knew she was deeply interested in his career; she would always follow it with pleasure. . . Meanwhile they were very happy as friends; and they couldn't be more than that now, could they ? He would be prudent, she knew, and they could continue to enjoy each other's society as they had these many years.

Here was as near an acceptance of his suit as any modest maiden could make before he was in a position to ask her father for her hand. Certainly she did not forbid his hoping; certainly she expressed herself as having a warm regard for him. More than this he could not ask; he would not have deemed her modest had she confessed to loving him.

While he had been uncertain of her reply he had questioned himself constantly; he assured himself over and over again that he expected too much of her; she could not reciprocate his feelings; she was an angel, he was only a struggling young lawyer, a scribbler of insignificant verse, a man with a crippled leg. And yet he could not forget her happy flush when he pressed her hand, her arch smiles, her friendly letters, her almost tender greetings and farewells. He could not feel but that he stood higher in her favor than any other man; she had never repressed his expressions of regard — he had not previous to this letter used the word *love*, but she could not have been ignorant of the depth of his feelings. She had not repulsed him; could it be that she would favor him ? And so when her reassuring letter came, his relief, his gratitude, his love were so strong that he burst into "a very hearty fit of crying." Instead of feeling vain and set up, he felt humble and unworthy.

As he read and reread his precious letter he began to wonder if he had overestimated the warmth of its expression. Ten times a day he would unfold and study it, ten times and more he would assure himself that it was indeed encouragement. Finally he felt the need of consulting some one who would tell him honestly if he were a conceited ass so to interpret it. He could not let anything so precious out of his possession; but he could and did make a fair copy which he sent to the friend who had advised him to put his fortune to the test. To his great joy his friend interpreted the missive exactly as he did himself, as "highly flattering and favourable."

Now the lad dreamed of his first meeting with Williamina. She would be coming back to town in two or three months. How would she greet him ? Would she receive him as warmly as he wished ? Would she kiss his letters as he now kissed hers ? Would she let him kiss her when they met ?

At last she came. They met; he kissed her hand; she blushed, and withdrew her fingers from his grasp; but she did not chide him. She spoke to him sweetly and seriously. She was fond of him, but of course as he knew himself there could be nothing between them *yet*. Meanwhile she was, he knew, always his sincere friend. So they went on, more intimate than before, though never avowed lovers; that could not be until he had had some measure of success. He began to publish his metrical translations of German verse, carrying his scanty laurels

to the sweetly smiling, gently appreciative Williamina.
He talked of Poesy and Art and Fame. She was an excellent listener.

Nevertheless she distributed her favors among many;
Walter must not think that he owned her; she liked him
*best;* but he needn't think that she liked him to the ex-
clusion of the rest of the world of young men. He
suffered jealous pangs, he had his moments of doubt;
he even thought her at times an insincere flirt; again he
would sternly reprove himself for the slightest disloyal
thought. He must not presume too far till he could
claim her openly. But for all that he believed that she
was his.

So matters stood for more than a year. Meanwhile
Williamina was well into her twenties, high time for a
girl to marry. Scott had not yet shown himself able
to support her in the approved style; and anyhow there
was no engagement between them. Her father and
mother talked the matter over. They had been warned
by Scott's father; they knew the lad's devotion.

"Pshaw," said Sir John. " 'Tis only puppy love. He'll
get over it. Ye're sure our Willie hasna lost her heart
to him ?"

"I've questioned her pretty thoroughly. Of course I
havena asked her direct. That wouldna do. But Willie's a good girl; she would want to please her father."

"Well, see what you can do. Sir William Forbes has
been speaking to me; he's wanting a wife, and a fine
match he is. He asked me today if he could meet our
Willie; he's thinking maybe she'd be the one for him."

"How old might Sir William be ? Are you sure he'd be good to the child ? What's his fortune ?"

Lady Jane had dozens of questions to ask before she could admit Sir William's eligibility. She demanded a meeting with him herself, and was favorably impressed.

Craftily she and her husband opened their campaign. In Willie's presence they praised Sir William, his looks, his carriage, his conversation, his wise use of his wealth. Having built up the picture of a paragon, they introduced him to her at an evening gathering. After the last guest had gone, Lady Jane lingered with her daughter to discuss their guests. Walter had been his usual boisterous self, but Lady Jane chose to think him noisier than usual. The other young men seemed also to lack poise beside the polish of Sir William. Didn't Willie notice that ? Oh, yes, Willie had noticed what a perfect gentleman Sir William was. And didn't his coat fit him admirably ? He had praised her singing very sympathetically; she was sure he understood music. And what a charming accent he had when he dropped into French now and then. He would be an addition to their parties this winter, a very pleasant addition.

Sir William came often. He brought new music for Willie to sing. He was no harum-scarum youngster to rush to her harp to turn the pages of her music unsolicited. At first he stood quietly at the other end of the room, watching the ostentatious devotion of Walter who constantly dashed to her side, to select a song, to tighten the harp strings, to lift a chair. Walter's voice rose bold and loud whenever there was a chorus to join.

Sir William acted the part of attentive listener. When he remained for dinner he handed Williamina to her place as if she were a duchess; no boyish nonsense, no giggling, no whispering. He listened to her faint speeches as if they were worth hearing; he paid her grave compliments that flattered her as much in their assumption of her being an adult and a lady, as in their intrinsic flattery. Walter spilled his devotion for all the world to see. Sir William let her see that his affection was a secret for her alone. He danced divinely, too; not the swaggering step of Walter's friends, not the undignified rapidity of these others, but a smooth stately motion that made for harmony.

Lady Jane used her opportunities. These boys had done very well to pass away idle time; she had herself enjoyed seeing Willie romp with them. A girl ought to have a good romping time before she settled down as sensible wife and mother; she wished her parents had realized that. Willie knew that her parents had never begrudged her a frolic. Still it was time to be thinking more seriously. Willie would not want to be forever frolicking with these youngsters. She would want to settle down soon. And she could not fail to be aware of Sir William's devotion.

Correct as his behavior was, Sir William had managed to convey to Willie the seriousness of his intentions; others, too, were suspicious. Many a time Walter Scott glared at him as he led Willie into the dance; many a time the two glowered at each other across the young lady's harp. Perhaps it was not always accidental that

Walter now and then, in his haste to reach the lady's side, bumped into Sir William. Hot words at times passed between them. Walter began to dream of duels, of all for love and the world well lost, of death, flight, and all the panoply of wounded love. But no duel came. The careful Williamina distributed her favors evenly; Walter loved, languished, hoped, despaired, and woke to hope again. Willie had never repudiated the half-promise of her letter; she would not play him false.

He did not know that canny Sir William, believing the time ripe for his proposal, had sounded out Lady Jane, not wishing to risk his dignity in a refusal from a young woman. Lady Jane hastened to write him a lengthy epistle, artlessly revealing to him how she had played his cards for him, carefully praising him after each visit, contrasting him constantly with these other swains, and leading Williamina on to echo her approbation. He might, she assured him, go ahead without fear.

Meanwhile Walter Scott after a summer of more or less satisfactory letters had come to the Stuarts' country home on an invitation of long standing. In spite of the fact that he had constantly witnessed the gracious reception of Sir William he had not really feared his rivalry; he was in love, Sir William was not. He hoped that Willie loved him; he knew that she did not love Sir William. Sometimes he feared her pliant disposition; she was if anything too ready to please. She might grow tired of waiting for her lover to grow rich; she might turn her fancy to please her parents. Walter could hardly be blind to the favor they showed Sir William. But he

was young; and he couldn't believe that prudent riches
would beat out ardent first love. He wanted to think
that Willie loved him as deeply as he loved her. Blithely
he packed up and gaily he journeyed to his doom. He
was received with an exaggerated courtesy which did its
best to ignore his expectation of a warmer reception.
After dinner Willie evaded him to take a stroll in the
moonlit garden with Sir William. Lady Jane looked
after the vanishing couple significantly.

"You're such an old friend of the family, Walter,"
she said confidingly, "that I don't mind telling you,
though of course it won't be announced until we get back
to town — Sir William and our Willie are affianced."

## II

WILLIAMINA STUART and her "dearest, dearest William"
were married in October 1796. Fourteen months later
Walter Scott was himself a happy Benedict.

And yet he had thought himself completely heart-
broken. He had gone for a wild solitary ride in the
Scotch highlands, his world a vacuum because it no
longer held his true love; she was false, she had never
loved him. But she had whispered tender words, she
had written tender letters, she had even written poems
to him! Was she all false? Had she been dissem-
bling? No, he would swear she had not. She did not
love this man she would marry; she married him because
he had a title and money and estates; she was not worthy
to be loved; she had broken his heart; he would never

love another; all women were false; she had deceived him; no, he had deceived himself; but she had led him on; his life was ruined; he would never get over this. In his old age he loved to think that he never did get over it; that his heart had been permanently "cracked"; that he had loved once and for all; that visions of his first love haunted his dreams.

Nevertheless the following February found him in the gayest of spirits, with his youthful friends organizing a body of volunteer cavalry to defend the country from the dreaded invasion of the French under Napoleon. Such happy young men rejoicing in military junketings and in uniforms of scarlet and gold, dreaded less than they hoped. They thoroughly enjoyed the bustle of organization, the election of officers — Scott was at first Paymaster, Quartermaster, and Secretary ! — the drilling heroically in early morning when they ordinarily would have luxuriated in bed, the admiration of the ladies, the patriotic fervor with which they offered to serve anywhere in England or Scotland, when the invasion should occur.

To Walter Scott, whose military longings had heretofore been thwarted by his lameness, the opportunity was golden. Years of hard riding had made him an excellent horsemen; he was tireless and fearless in the saddle; none of his cronies could outride him. He fairly burst with military zeal. His conversation smacked of nothing these days but pistols, swords, cartouche-boxes, horse-pickers, hussar-boots, holsters, drills, and counter-charges. "Scott," declared one of his fellow lawyers, "is

SIR WALTER SCOTT

*From a painting by Sir Henry Raeburn*

become the merest trooper that ever was begotten by a drunken dragoon on his trull in a hay-loft. Not an idea crosses his mind, or a word his lips, that has not an allusion to some d—d instrument or evolution of the Cavalry — 'Draw your swords — by single files to the right of front — to the left wheel-charge !' "

He was so overjoyed with his new occupation that his merriment could hardly be contained. In the intervals of rest after each exercise of the morning drill he would perform comic antics on his horse, Lenore (named for the German ballad which he had translated for his first literary production), shouting out broad jokes, until his comrades were reduced to tears of laughter. At the officers' mess he was even less restrained; story, joke, and song flowed from his quick lips; he was the public entertainer. *Earl Walter,* his companions called him, partly in affection, partly in fun; for not only did he assume leadership wherever possible, but he was known to have the strongest feeling of ancestor worship; he cherished his descent from Scotch lairds and worthies more tenderly than any genuine earl. If his heart was broken past mending, he concealed his sorrow well. Williamina was married; and Walter was cavorting in the best of spirits with his friends, decking himself out in the grandest of uniforms, riding about conscious of the admiring glances cast at this handsome big soldier well seated on a magnificent prancing steed.

The next summer he set off cheerfully on a walking tour with his brother, John, and another young man, Adam Ferguson. He may have sighed now and then;

he may have been a bit cynical on the subject of love and women, but he was a merry companion, always ready for fun and frolic.  He even wrote a pensive poem to a young lady he met on his travels, for whom he certainly had at least a passing fancy.  Then one day, on a long walk with his friend, he saw a black-haired beauty ride past on horseback.  Without intruding on her they increased their pace, watching to learn her destination. Both youths were indeed pleased to see her turn in and alight at their own inn.  That night they donned their scarlet uniforms, adjusted the gold trimmings, saw to it that their boots had been given an extra polish, squared their shoulders, and marched to the ballroom.  Sure enough the beauty was there, already the centre of a knot of admirers.  They sought for an introduction. Soon Walter had the pleasure of gazing into a pair of fine brown eyes and listening to a sweet low voice marked by just enough French accent to make it pleasing.

This young refugee had all the animation of her race, combined with a pretty reserve which showed her rather unused to society.  John and Ferguson were equally captivated; they were quick to secure dances.  Walter, once more saddened over his inability to dance, had learned never to mope over his misfortune; the years of attendance on Williamina had taught him that popular young ladies danced with many men, but they sat and talked to few.  And he could, he knew, talk interestingly; had not Edinburgh belles — and Willie herself — been always ready to sit out dances with him ?  He could not ask a new acquaintance to sit out dances, but he could and did secure her hand for the supper. He exerted himself to please; he fancied that he succeeded.

Next day his brother gave him interesting details of the young lady's circumstances. She was the daughter of Jean Charpentier, a French royalist who had prudently invested part of his fortune in England at the first alarm of the Revolution. He had died soon after, and his wife had with her son and daughter fled to England to put themselves under the protection of the Marquis of Downshire. The marquis had been moved by his friendship with M. Charpentier to act as guardian to the children when their mother died. Part of the children's income came, indeed, from his lordship since their father had invested some of his capital in a mortgage on the Downshire estates. At his recommendation they had anglicized their name into Carpenter. Charles, the brother of Charlotte, had been given an excellent appointment with the East India Company. He was in sole possession of his father's fortune, but as he was unmarried and also very fond of his sister, he granted her a generous income. Estimates of his fortune and her income varied, gossip exaggerating both. Actually Charlotte Carpenter had at this time from her brother five hundred pounds a year, enough to make her an excellent match from Scott's point of view, though the fact that her income was dependent upon her brother's whim made his father think it a precarious fortune.

For it was only the briefest time before Scott was asking his parents' consent to his engagement. Never

had he raved over Williamina as he now did over Charlotte. He said, of course, that this was different, this
was the sober love of a disappointed man — he felt called
upon to explain to Charlotte just how disappointed and
betrayed he had been — this was not the unearthly glow
of first love. For instance, he was willing to admit that
she wasn't the most beautiful woman in the world. Of
course she was the prettiest in any gathering in which he
saw her. He didn't believe he would commit suicide
if she wouldn't have him; but then he believed she
would have him.

He was so thoroughly absorbed in her that he soon
put his fortune to the test. Very honorably he told her
his income, his expectations, the cracked state of his
heart. That he was head over heels in love Charlotte
could easily see. As for her, she had lost her heart to
him at the very outset; he was so big, so gentle, so entertaining, so merry; and it was such a pity he was lame.
Of course they could not consider themselves engaged
until he had consulted his parents and she Lord Downshire — she was of legal age, but he stood in her father's
place and she would not marry against his wishes. Scott
lost no time in writing a long letter to his mother, pre-
senting his suit. He was hard put to it to restrain his
exuberance; Williamina had rejected him, and this paragon among maidens had found him worthy to be loved.
He assured his mother that this time he had consulted
his "judgment" as well as his affections. He was, in
truth, no longer a silly boy; he had just passed his
twenty-sixth birthday. The match was not so hasty as

she might think, for whereas they had known each other only a short time, that time had been spent in unusual intimacy at this watering place where they had been living in the same house.   His Charlotte was, fortunately, a Protestant.

Back with his cronies he was, so one testified, "sair beside himself about Miss Carpenter; — we toasted her twenty times over — and sat together, he raving about her, until it was one in the morning."

The first letter he received from his Charlotte was far more satisfactory than all he had ever had from the false Williamina:

Carlisle, October 4, 1797
It is only an hour since I received Lord Downshire's letter. You will say, I hope, that I am indeed very good to write so soon, but I almost fear that all my goodness can never carry me through all this plaguy writing.   Lord Downshire will be happy to hear from you.   He is the very best man on earth — his letter is kind and affectionate, and full of advice, much in the style of *your last*.   I am to consult *most carefully my heart*.   Do you believe I did not do it when I gave you my consent ?   It is true, I don't like to reflect on that subject.   I am afraid.   It is very awful to think it is for life. How can I ever laugh after such tremendous thoughts ?   I believe never more.   I am hurt to find that your friends don't think the match a prudent one.   If it is not agreeable to them all, you must then forget me, for I have too much pride to think of connecting myself in a family were I not equal to them.   Pray, my dear sir, write to Lord D. immediately — explain yourself to him as you would to me, and he will, I am sure, do all he can to serve us.   If you really love me, you must love him, and write to him as you would to a friend.
Adieu, — au plaisir de vous revoir bientôt.
C. C.

In those careful days one didn't *tutoyer* one's betrothed.

Four days from the time Charlotte dated her letter Scott was on his way to visit her in Carlisle, his lordship's letter, giving his consent, safely buttoned in his coat pocket. He would like to have carried his Charlotte off posthaste, but she was reluctant to such hurry. He wrote mournfully that he supposed he would have to wait for the Christmas holidays, more than two months off.

His impatience was such upon his return that he tortured himself when Charlotte did not answer his letters by return post. Charlotte chided him:

Your last letter, my dear sir, contains a very fine train of *perhaps,* and of so many pretty conjectures, that it is not flattering you to say you excel in the art of tormenting yourself. As it happens, you are quite wrong in all your suppositions. I have been waiting for Lord D.'s answer to your letter, to give a full answer to your very proper enquiries about my family. Miss Nicholson [her companion-governess] says that when she did offer to give you some information, you refused it — and advises me *now* to wait for Lord D.'s letter. Don't believe I have been idle; I have been writing very long letters to him, and all about you. How can you think that I will give an answer about the house until I hear from London? — that is quite impossible; and I believe you are a little out of your senses to imagine I can be in Edinburgh before the twelfth of next month. O, my dear sir, no — you must not think of it this *great while.* . . *Sans adieu,*

C. C.

Three days later she scolded him roundly:

Indeed, Mr. Scott, I am by no means pleased with all this writing. I have told you how much I dislike it, and yet you still persist in asking me to write, and that by return of post. O, you really are quite out of your senses. I should not have indulged you in that whim of yours, had you not given me that hint that my silence gives an air of mystery. I have no reason that can detain me in acquainting you that my father and mother were French, of the name of Charpentier; he had a place under government; their residence was at Lyons, where you would find on enquiries that they lived in good repute and in *very good style*. I had the misfortune of losing my father before I could know the value of such a parent. At his death we were left to the care of Lord D., who was his very great friend; and very soon after I had the affliction of losing my mother. Our taking the name of Carpenter was on my brother's going to India, to prevent any little difficulties that might have occurred. I hope now you are pleased. Lord D. could have given you every information, as he has been acquainted with all my family. You say you almost love *him;* but until your *almost* comes to a *quite* I cannot love *you*. Before I conclude this famous epistle, I will give you a little hint — that is, not to put so many *must* in your letters — it is beginning *rather too soon;* and another thing is, that I take the liberty not to mind them much, but I expect you mind me. You *must* take care of yourself; you *must* think of me, and believe me yours sincerely,

C. C.

Even the path of second love did not run quite smoothly. Walter's father and mother were perturbed over his ardor, fearful lest he be laying himself open to a new disappointment. They were canny people; this girl was, after all, French; and she had no assured fortune; her income was dependent upon her brother who might at any moment marry, or grow tired of sending substantial sums to a distant sister. Walter's earnings were obviously not enough to support a fashionable wife.

From John's account they were aware of the young lady's delight in society. She would want to keep a carriage — she had told Walter so. She was used to a somewhat broader scale of living than he; she had after all been brought up by a marquis. The old folks shook their heads; they weren't sure of the wisdom of this match for a boy who had shown himself too much at the mercy of the fair.

His letters became gloomy; he could not conceal from Charlotte the opposition he met, especially since her sympathy was dear to him. There was, too, a feeling in his mind that she must not think, because of her larger income — he could not earn that much in a year were he to try ever so hard — that she was a great prize for him. He suggested gloomily that they had better emigrate to one of England's colonies; they could better make their fortune there; or at least conceal from their friends their restricted mode of living so that her friends would not pity her for having married a poor man.

Charlotte dismissed the plea of poverty lightly; she could not worry over a state of which she had never had any experience; nor was she likely to for all his forebodings. Charles would continue to be generous; had he not already promised to increase her income? Was not the whole sum secured to her for the next year already? She wrote Scott to put aside such thoughts. "Depend on yourself and your profession," she urged. "I have no doubt you will rise very high, and be a *great rich man.*"

No one had ever told him that before; he had been told that he was talented, that he had a pretty gift for rhyming, that he handled his law work fairly well; his friends had said that they expected great things of him, but no one had said as Charlotte did that he would "rise very high, and be a great rich man." He would be worthy of her trust; he *would* be great and rich; how he did not know, but he *would*. He would justify her faith in him. Pretty little thing ! He wasn't going to see her deprived of the pleasures of society. As she wrote herself, she did "love any thing that is *stylish.*" She wanted to keep her own carriage though she was willing to wait a bit. By George ! she shouldn't have to wait long. She should have pretty stylish things, she should have her carriage. She shouldn't have to trouble her pretty head with economies. She had been so very grave when he visited her in November. She apologized in her first letter after his return:

I don't know what could be the matter with me, I was so very low, and felt really ill: it was even a trouble to speak. The settling of our little plans — all looked so much in earnest — that I began reflecting more seriously than I generally do, or *approve of.* I don't think that very thoughtful people ever can be happy. As this is my maxim, adieu to all thoughts.

And she enclosed a lock of her raven hair.

Yet she almost repented of having accepted Walter's gift of a miniature of himself. She feared that his father

was seriously prejudiced against her as a French girl.
She wrote:

I am certain your father and uncle say that you are a hot
*heady* young man, quite mad, I assure you I join with them
if you talk of going to the West Indies; and I must believe,
that when you have such an idea, you have then determined
to think no more of me.

She knew perfectly well that he would only think of
her the more.  He liked being called a "hot heady young
man."  Perhaps he was; he was certainly mad about
her.  He didn't want one of your sensible, steady, housekeeping wives; he wanted this girl all sparkle and high
spirits, to whom it would always be a delight to come
home.  Suppose she didn't count the sheets and dole out
the tea; they'd be above cheeseparing fast enough !  He
would find a way to make money for her.  She made
no pretences, she laid no claim to great common sense:

If I could but really believe that my letter gave you only
half the pleasure you express, I should almost think, my dearest Scott, that I should get very fond of writing merely for the
pleasure to *indulge* you — that is saying a great deal.  I hope
you are sensible of the compliment I pay you, and don't expect I shall *always* be so pretty behaved.  You may depend on
me, my dearest friend, for fixing as *early* a day as I possibly
can; and if it happens to be not quite so soon as you wish,
you must not be angry with me.  It is very unlucky you are
such a bad housekeeper — as I am no better.  I shall try.  I hope
to have very soon the pleasure of seeing you, and to tell you
how much I love you; but I wish the first fortnight was over.
With all my love, and those sort of pretty things — adieu.

CHARLOTTE.

P. S. *Etudiez votre Français.*  Remember you are to teach
me Italian in return, but I shall be but a stupid scholar.
*Aimez Charlotte.*

Four days later she named the date for him to come to Carlisle for the marriage. "Oh, my dear Scott, on that day I shall be yours for ever." The solemnity of that thought did not prevent her vanity from peeking out in a postscript when she thought of meeting her new relatives for the first time:

P. S. Arrange it so that we shall see none of your family on the night of our arrival. I shall be so tired, and such a fright, I should not be seen to advantage.

On the day before Christmas 1797, Walter Scott, four months after his twenty-sixth birthday, led Charlotte Carpenter to the altar, successful at last in love as he meant from now on to be in all things.

# CHAPTER II

*As for poetry, it is very little labor to me.*
                                    WALTER SCOTT.

## CHAPTER II

WHEN Charlotte had expressed to her "dearest Scott" her reluctance to exchange her gay free girlhood for the responsibilities of marriage, to settle down as a matron in Edinburgh where she did not know a single person besides himself, Walter had written most persuasively to his "smart-looking little girl with dark brown hair" that there were plenty of amusements in the city and that it would be the study of his life to prevent her feeling "one moment's *Ennui*." Accordingly he entered into a series of social evenings, introducing his pretty bride to his fellow lawyers and fellow troopers.

All the more because he had the year before worn his broken heart upon his sleeve, did Scott rejoice in his friends' frank admiration of his little French wife. To her delight she found these lawyers were not grave grey-beards, but such young people as she had always danced and played among. Their evenings were full of variety, their fun often boisterous. She need not yet assume matronly dignity and sit in a corner.

And her dear Scott loved the theatre almost as much as she did herself. She dressed her prettiest, knowing that he loved to show her off. He was pleased to appear before the world — and Williamina — as a lucky suitor, husband of as dainty a little parcel of femininity as Edinburgh had ever seen.

As her modesty had shrunk from the selection of a house before marriage, Scott took her first to elegant lodgings where to the horror of the landlady she constantly and "not on high occasions merely," sat in the drawingroom. Bubbling with mirth Charlotte mimicked the good woman's scandalized reproach thinking to amuse her mother-in-law. She ended her recital with a gust of laughter in which the elder Mrs. Scott did not join. Sitting very straight — never could it be said of her that her back touched a chair ! — she frowned at her frivolous daughter-in-law until the ill-considered merry laugh died away. Though she never became intimate enough for actual reproof, she had difficulty in restraining her disapproval of such levity. Charlotte seemed to her more decorative than became the wife of a young lawyer. Perhaps time and responsibility would turn her into a sober matron.

Walter himself had nothing to complain of; he was the envy of his friends; he had an attractive companion for all his gaieties; he who had been pitied and even scorned when Williamina deserted him, now stood before the world, a happy man.

In the summer he carried Charlotte off to a romantic thatched cottage at Lasswade, six miles from town, a cottage nestling in a few acres of meadow and woodland close to the River Esk. The road that led to its grounds was a winding one lined with hedges of hawthorn. Already Scott saw himself as a country gentleman, occupied

with the improvement of an estate. Though the estate
was small to begin with, there were plenty of embellish-
ments to be made. Charlotte sentimentally longed for
a rustic arbor; perhaps one could be managed at the
gate to their grounds. At either side of the gate grew
lithe young willow trees. Scott surveyed them critically.
This was his first landscaping; it must be thought out.
With infinite care he experimented, measured, trimmed,
cut and calculated, Charlotte watching and praising.
He examined the tools in the shed, ran his finger over
axe blades, tested the teeth of the old saw. He could do
nothing until these things were sharpened. Sharpened
they were, and a fine piece of new wood prepared for
the slaughter. Charlotte's astonishment at his skill was
gratifying; he would show her what kind of man she
had married ! The wooden crosspiece was made, the
willows were firmly united, and Charlotte had her pretty
arch over the gate. That night they strolled out into the
moonlit garden, down the rose-bordered path to the gate,
to stand admiringly under the arch, his arm about her
waist, his lips meeting hers after each murmured endear-
ment. The night grew late. Slowly they withdrew to
the house, walking backwards to keep in view the moonlit arch, the work of his hands, the first fruits of his
proprietorship.

Exuberant over his success he turned to the manu-
facture of a diningroom table which should meet Charlotte's somewhat exacting requirements. With a bit of
sewing in her dainty hands, his little French bride sat
under the trees, watching him. Again and again he

would have to discard his tools, sit at her feet to tell her how sweet she was.

Even these activities were not enough for his exuberant health and spirits. He rode hard, choosing his time at first when Charlotte was resting or taking tea with new-made friends. He would head his horse down steep cliffs, plunge headlong into the turbulent waters of a dangerous ford and be up and off again before his companion, if he chanced to have one, finished his Halloa of fright. He took long walks, scrambling along banks, unperturbed by scratches or tumbles. He was incurably adventure-some, eternally boyish. He described himself to a correspondent who had never seen him as "a rattle-sculled half-lawyer, half-sportsman, through whose head a regiment of horse has been exercising since he was five years old; half-educated — half-crazy, as his friends sometimes tell him; half everything. . ."

His Charlotte could not, of course, accompany him on his walks and rides; she had to watch him go off with male companions, and learn not to expect him back until dinners were cold with waiting. She could not go because for one thing the athletic woman was yet to be discovered; and because she was now properly in what was called "delicate health." In those days there was no prudishness about the matter; Scott hastened to communicate his good fortune and his delight to all. The married sisters of his friends amused themselves and him by writing to him their prophecies of the child's future; they speculated upon his main inheritance: would he be more antiquary than poet ? would he lisp verses in his cradle ? would he be philosopher or hero ? If he were the true son of his sire he would surely combine hero and poet. It is quite plain that Scott shared his verses with his friends and that they were not blind to his frustrated desire to be a military hero. But the child, born in October, lived only a day.

In the year that intervened before the birth of the next child (a girl), Scott did his best to keep Charlotte busy and happy. He carried her off to London with him in the spring, there to renew the delight he had had in his only previous visit twenty odd years ago. Like two children they went about enjoying everything from the stories they gathered at the Tower to the latest plays and the acquaintanceship of literary people.

For Scott had at last really entered the literary field with his translation of *Götz von Berlichingen*. His earlier quarto of translations starting from the privately printed *Lenore* which Edinburgh appreciated less than did Williamina Stuart, its inspirer, and of which London failed even to be aware, had been a still birth. Whatever his disappointment, Scott had spent no time brooding; military zeal, courtship, and marriage had filled his days; and his enjoyment of ballads went on undimmed. His friends shared his enthusiasm; perhaps in time the public would come to listen to him.

And then he met Matthew Lewis. The public which had neglected *Lenore* had snatched with avidity Lewis's romance *The Monk* which satisfied at once the popular appetite for ghostly surprises, and its more legitimate interest in ballads. "Monk" Lewis became a drawing-

room idol.  Fashionable London passed him on to the
socially élite of Edinburgh.   And Scott, big healthy man,
felt drawn at first sight to this diminuitive dandy and
literary lion.   Little men were ever to hold an attraction
for Scott; perhaps because subconsciously he felt their
littleness a handicap for them comparable to his lameness for him.   He was larger than most men; only his
lameness gave him a sense of inferiority.   These men
were physically normal but they were inferior in
stature.

Lewis was equally impressed with the bigness, the
vigor, the enthusiasm, and most of all the admiration of
Scott.   Here was a man made to his hand.   For Lewis
was busily pushing his success with the public by gathering *Tales of Wonder* for which he sadly needed contri-
butions.   This brawny Scotchman was grist for his mill.
Scott's delight at seeing his own poetical translations in
print in Lewis's miscellany was pleasant to see.   Lewis,
not ill pleased to be the patron of a handsome giant,
negotiated with a bookseller for the publication of Scott's
translation of *Götz von Berlichingen*.   Now Scott could
bring to his happy wife a real volume with his name
on the title page.   Together they could appreciate the
significance of his being at last a recognized author.
And though the profit was hardly worth mentioning,
still it was something; the bookseller had actually paid
twenty-five guineas for the copyright.   In London Scott
and his wife basked in the sunshine of literary people,
dreaming of the day when the name of Walter Scott
would embellish the title pages of many books.

For Scott's heart had never been in his profession; winning a lawsuit had never held for him the satisfaction of tracking down one romantic ballad. Tales of daring, tales of horror, anything romantic and full of action pleased him more than a fee, though he performed his legal duties meticulously. Nevertheless he had not that enjoyment of his profession which, as he well knew, was the path to advancement in it. Moreover the business which had come to him through his father's office was showing a decline. His father had resigned the management to a son who not only did not keep the business up to its former efficiency but in the course of years ran it to the ground. Meanwhile the father was very ill. At times he seemed himself, but for the most part he lay or sat propped up in a chair in a sort of lethargy from which he would rouse to reproach his dutiful and gentle daughter for some fancied neglect. His death came during Scott's spring in London.

What Scott lost in business through his brother's lack of good management, he gained in a direct inheritance which, though not large, made his financial position more secure. He knew that he could not forever rely on the increased generosity of his brother-in-law who might at any time marry and have dependents (he did marry some half-dozen years later). It was therefore with something of relief that he received his appointment as sheriff-depute with an assured salary of three hundred pounds a year. He now had to maintain a house in Edinburgh as well as the summer cottage at Lasswade; and less and less did he curb his hospitable nature. He dearly loved to surround himself with guests, especially in the country where he seemed a sort of laird. Guests made necessary more servants and an enlarged way of living. And now that Charlotte was having children fairly frequently she really did need the carriage for which she had always longed. It was in the summer of 1800 that she was able to go abroad in her own carriage, a phaeton "at once strong, and low, and handsome," its cost within thirty guineas according to Scott's specification. He had taken an enormous pleasure in thus gratifying her; and a delight in astonishing the natives; for this was the first wheeled carriage the countryside had ever seen. His wife rode about like a titled lady; that was as it should be. A "great rich man" had been her prophecy for him; he would not disappoint her. He was not yet thirty and already he had satisfied one of her ambitious longings. There were many years ahead in which he would accomplish all that she could desire.

As his income increased then, his expenses increased. Upon obtaining the sheriffdom Scott had immediately set about making the cottage at Lasswade more elegant; before long he decided that Charlotte must have a larger and finer town house; people who kept a carriage ought to live in a more fashionable quarter of Edinburgh. With his usual optimism he foresaw large returns from his literary labors which were now bringing out volumes of Scotch Minstrelsy.

*The Minstrelsy of the Scottish Border* sprang naturally from the insatiable curiosity that from his earliest childhood had sought out legend and song about the chief-

tains, his ancestors. Having given over countless hours
to the transcribing of ballads he felt the urge to see
them in print, especially after his kind reception by the
literary figures of London. *Götz von Berlichingen* was a
book, to be sure, with his name on the title page, but
for all that it was only a translation. When he rescued
from oblivion the legends of the Scotch Border he was
more nearly creating literature. For his work went beyond mere compilation; he had himself composed ballads, original verses based on current legend. And these
efforts of his were not, so his friends averred, unworthy
to stand among the ancient ballads. They were in the
true Scotch tradition; though new-minted they bore the
stamp of age.

The two volumes which appeared in 1802 were more
definitely his own than any translation could be. He
had every right to be proud of his authorship. Handsome
volumes, too, he thought them, printed as he had stipu-
lated to the publisher by his old friend and schoolfellow
James Ballantyne of Kelso. The public would surely
appreciate these ballads at their true worth; here were
romance, mystery, chivalry, all soundly based on legends
that had their roots in Scottish history. The public did
not disappoint his expectations; an edition of eight hundred copies was soon exhausted, and a third volume was
called for.

As he could now earn considerable money with his
pen, doing indeed what he most loved to do, he could
with confidence look forward to an income really suitable
for Charlotte and her growing family. He had for

some time cherished the idea of giving up law altogether, and with some clerkship added to his office of sheriff-depute would have enough to live well upon with the sure success of his pen.

Meanwhile for the moment things were not going quite so well. His chief, Lord Napier, chose to insist upon his fulfilling the letter of his obligations as sheriff by residing in his jurisdiction a part of every year; his lordship went so far as to threaten to report him to the government if he continued to summer in Lasswade, and if he devoted so much of his time with his beloved cavalry troop, that volunteer troop which was always keyed up to the defence of the realm from French invasion, and which meantime enjoyed drills, and uniforms, dinners and parties, and summer encampments. Lord Napier's suggestion that he resign from this troop of volunteers found Scott quite deaf.

This troop was the very breath of the lame officer's life. They were all valiant young men of good family, mounted on superb horses, beautifully accoutred. That they thrilled with delight at each rumor of invasion is certain; they longed to prove that their military ardor was justified, that their equipment was more than a magnificent toy. Scott made his own justification: "For myself, I must own that to one who has, like myself, *la tête un peu exaltée,* the 'pomp and circumstance of war' gives, for a time, a very poignant and pleasing sensation. The imposing appearance of cavalry, in particular, and the rush which marks their onset, appear to me to partake highly of the sublime."

When, a little later, Edinburgh was practically trans-
formed into an armed camp, his spirits were jubilant.
He went about, like other militant lawyers, with his
uniform under his gown. Even shopkeepers served their
customers clad in scarlet. The presence of a large gar-
rison of regular troops stimulated the patriotism and im-
proved the military appearance of the ten thousand
volunteers. When the volunteers were permitted to engage in sham battles and sieges, feelings rose to a high
pitch. Officers had trouble separating the combatants.
Such joy did these soldiers take in their warfare, such
zest did they show for butchering their fellowmen that
again and again the battles came close to reality. Com-
panies could not be made to hold to the prearranged programme when their own defeat was scheduled. Marches,
countermarches, charges, pursuits, sieges, ambuscades;
war was a great game; it was a pity it could not be played
in firm reality. Said Scott: ". . . so great is the present
military zeal, that I really wish our rulers would devise
some way of calling it into action, were it only on the
economical principle of saving so much good courage
from idle evaporation."

There was no invasion, and Scott participated in nothing but sham battles. His own military ardor was not,
however, wasted. If he could not himself fight the good
fight, he could and did in the years to come carry his
heroes through battle and danger to triumphant success.
It was through his own creations that Scott realized his
life's hopes; he could not himself, lame giant, serve his
country; he could not overcome the enemy, he could

not sheath his sword after a valiant fight; but he could
do all these things vicariously in the persons of his own
literary creations. The type of literature to which he
turned was definitely determined by the frustration of
his own ambition. Lame he could not be a conqueror;
but pen in hand he could seek adventure, rescue the un-
fortunate, fight valiantly, pursue the gleam of glory.
More and more did he develop his imaginary world;
more and more did his imagination create for him situa-
tions which in actual life could never be his.

So far he had been translating, collecting; he had fer-
reted out ballads, tales of wonder, anything of marvel
and action. He was working toward original balladry,
romances of his own weaving. He had tried out his
powers in reworking old ballads and in reassembling in
verse ancient legends in his *Border Minstrelsy,* but it was
not until 1805 that he finally published a complete long
poem of his own. In the world of romance where his
mind most loved to dwell he visualized himself as the
survivor of the minstrels, a late-born singer whose pitch
yet harmonized with the melodies of bygone days. And
as the world had listened to the minstrels, so it would
listen to him. The tale he sang was old and yet new;
it was fresh as country dew; surely the public would
find it refreshing after years of citified, stiff, correct heroic
couplets. The verse which slipped from his pen was
smoother and easier than anything that had appeared
from the presses for a long time. Here was a romantic
story easier to read than prose; it poured itself upon the
page enticing the reader like a pleasant mountain stream.

Yet even his confidence was amazed when *The Lay of the Last Minstrel* met with immediate success, making poetry profitable merchandise. The seven hundred and fifty handsome quartos which made up the first edition merely whetted the public appetite. Edition followed edition in quick succession; in time Scott could indeed flatter himself that he understood the literary market, for what other poet could count his sales in the thirty thousands ? Here were popularity, fame, fortune. A great rich man Charlotte had said. Well, here was the first step toward greatness and riches. Though he sold the copyright, thereby losing future royalties, his profits were nearly eight hundred pounds, no small sum for a new poet. He had leapt into the class of best sellers. Immediately publishers made huge offers for his next poetical romance. Hardly had he begun *Marmion* when he had its purchase price of a thousand guineas in his hand.

Never had money arrived more opportunely. This new star in the poetical firmament was at this time involved in the most unpoetical and grilling legal toil. It was not even in his own proper field as a lawyer, mere attorney's work. Scotland, like England, sharply differentiated the work and training of lawyer and attorney; the elder Scott had brought up his son Thomas to his own trade of attorney but had educated Walter for the bar. Cannily he had, however, instructed the youth carefully in all the intricacies of his own attorney's business. Hence when Thomas got into serious difficulties it was his brother Walter who was called upon to disentangle him. Thomas had speculated unfortunately; moreover his management of the huge estates of Lord Abercorn had not run smoothly. He had muddled into a mire of debt. Walter took up the task of investigating attorney; with the utmost patience and thoroughness he plodded through mountains of papers, finally setting the Abercorn affairs straight without the expected loss of *Marmion's* fee which could then be applied toward settling Thomas abroad. It was indeed fortunate that he had been able to command such a sum.

Meanwhile his own household was increasingly expensive. He had given up Lasswade at Lord Napier's warning, and had settled at Ashestiel on the southern bank of the Tweed River, within his jurisdiction as sheriff. Ashestiel was a fair-sized estate owned by a cousin. To it Scott added a small sheep farm, going gravely into the scientific study of sheep-raising though his only object was to provide mutton for his own table. It was wisdom to raise as much food as possible on an estate which was seven miles from town.

The house stood on a bank high above the Tweed which in storm and flood was a raging torrent, and therefore doubly dear to Scott who seemed now as in childhood to thrive on perils. He would take his guests salmon-fishing by torchlight, escaping both burning and drowning through no caution of his. He would ride through the turbulent waters, fall off in midstream, and attempt the ford again as soon as he had been hauled ashore and wrung dry. He lamented the lack of wild forests and the comparatively small number of ancient trees that grew along the slopes of the ravine below the house. Down that ravine he slid more than once, to pick himself up at the river's brink to hallo to his startled companions as if it were but a pleasant start to the day's sport. He was still incurably daring, incurably boyish.

Ashestiel, though none too large, was still an estate on which he could play laird. The comfortable, commodious house looked out upon broad terraced walks running through a fine old-fashioned garden bordered with holly hedges. All about were mountains. The grand scenery, Scott would assure his city friends, was alone worth the trouble of a visit. He had no trouble convincing his friends; the house was constantly filled with guests. Anyone who would ride with him, or would prowl around out of doors was boisterously welcome.

He had not become really great yet, but he was beginning to be well known; he had not become really rich yet, but he was beginning to be well set up. His income, independent of his practice as a lawyer, was at this time somewhere around a thousand pounds a year, no small sum in the early nineteenth century. From a bachelor uncle he now inherited an estate which he sold profitably. Fortune was certainly looking up. These poems which the public appreciated so profitably were a joy to write. He often composed whole sections as he rode about on cavalry manœuvres. They were a mine of gold. Moreover he could now sell literary essays at a profitable price, and, best of all, he had a business scheme which, by the investment of this inheritance, could be made to repay him a hundredfold.

Scott's interest in the printing business sprang from what was perhaps his greatest interest, greater than his love of horses, dogs, military prowess, physical activities, romance, ancestor worship, even success and wealth, his interest in people. To the rescue of friends in distress he was always the first to arrive. To friends climbing the road to success he was ever ready with help and suggestion, especially if those friends were in any way associated with his youth.

He had at one time, during a health sojourn in Kelso, been a schoolfellow of James Ballantyne who had been attentive listener to the romantic tales the boy Walter Scott had loved to weave. James Ballantyne was now set up as a printer in Kelso. In 1800 Scott tempted him to remove to Edinburgh with prospects "of a very flattering nature." With characteristic thoroughness Scott investigated the printing field in Edinburgh, to report that there were three branches open, for all of which he felt confident that his old schoolfellow was fitted: the editorship of "a newspaper, which shall contain something of an uniform historical deduction of events, distinct from the farrago of detached and unconnected plagiarisms from the London paragraphs of 'The Sun' "; second, the publication of a magazine or two, and along with these the publication of law papers, accounts of Sessions, etc., this later a well-paid business; and finally, the publication of ancient and modern literature. The only printer of books then in town was, according to Scott, in very poor health; moreover, he was a very inferior printer. Ballantyne, he knew, was an excellent printer, one whose taste and performance were equally trustworthy. Here in Edinburgh there was, urged Scott, "a fair road to an ample fortune," upon which apparently Ballantyne had only to set his foot with firm and steady tread.

It did not occur to Scott that he had outlined enough activities for half a dozen men. His own mental and physical vigor were so great that he was happiest when he had on hand more tasks than a normal man could accomplish in five years, tasks which he would jovially attack, now one, now another, until one year saw them all neatly finished. He worked at top speed himself, throwing himself into each project with a wholehearted concentration that made mock of difficulties. He could not, seemingly, distinguish between his own wolfish appetite for work and the more dainty appetite of other men. He could himself have run a printing plant, published new editions of old works, new editions of current literature, managed two magazines and written their editorials, without retiring from the bar. Had he not been more interested in creating literature for Ballantyne to print he might have undertaken active supervision of this combination of enterprises he thrust upon his less talented friend.

It was in 1800 that Scott made this modest proposal; two years later James Ballantyne was comfortably settled in Edinburgh liberally financed by a loan from Scott.

Having brought Ballantyne to Edinburgh, Scott felt more than a friendly interest in his fortunes. He was too generous to give thought to the loan he had made him; money had come for his own needs too rapidly for him to be parsimonious; but he felt a responsibility for the success of Ballantyne's printing venture. He therefore recommended his press on all occasions, turning toward it all possible business, legal and literary. The press did good work; Ballantyne's taste and performance were always creditable. The press must be fed with more and more undertakings. Scott was always excellent at thinking up things to do. His mind fairly bubbled with literary schemes. Old authors needed editing, new editions were called for, the literary field had scarcely been scratched. Scott infected both Ballantyne and the booksellers (who were apparently aware of no connection other than friendly of Scott and Ballantyne) with his own enthusiasm. All sorts of literary projects were rushed through, without due regard for their financial success. Scott was so sure of Ballantyne's prosperity, so certain that through this business enterprise fortune large enough even to suit Charlotte would be gained, that he was jubilant indeed. He saw his way clear to retire from the bar, keeping his two offices of sheriff and clerk. As a matter of fact his legal business had steadily declined with his increasing literary labors. He now felt that it would be absurd to buy a mountain farm with his uncle's legacy; he would invest the money in the safest possible place, in a venture that would at once secure fortune to his friend and to himself. He would become a partner in Ballantyne's printing business. Through his loan he had already acquired a financial interest in the press; again Ballantyne was in sore need of new funds to enlarge the business fittingly. Why should he not invest his money as a shareholder, instead of advancing another inadequate loan? A loan made Ballantyne his debtor; an investment made him his partner. There is no more fascinating idea in the mind of man than that of benefiting oneself at the same time that one acts fairy godmother. Ballantyne's gratitude and appreciation were quite what he had pictured them. Scott spent a happy spring at Ashestiel thinking up great schemes.

A complete edition of British Poets, "at least a hundred volumes, to be published at the rate of ten a-year," "There is a scheme for you!" Johnson's was, after all, imperfect as well as out of print, Bell's suffered the same defects, and Anderson's which was the most complete as far as mere numbers went, was "contemptible in execution both of the editor and printer." Scott himself agreed to undertake Dryden, so that we owe to his enthusiasm for Ballantyne's press and his eagerness for its financial success, an invaluable scholastic achievement.

The eighteen volumes of Dryden took long to prepare, though Scott did not readily yield to the suggestions that he expurgate the text. Dryden, it was urged upon him, had written for bread, and had "poured forth more nonsense of indecency, particularly in his theatrical compositions, than almost any scribbler in that scribbling age."

In the interests of exact scholarship Scott replied:

I will not castrate John Dryden. I would as soon castrate my own father, as I believe Jupiter did of yore. What would you say to any man who would castrate Shakespeare, or Massinger, or Beaumont and Fletcher? I don't say but that it may be very proper to select correct passages for the use of boarding schools and colleges, being sensible no improper ideas can be suggested in these seminaries, unless they are intruded or smuggled under the beards and ruffs of our old dramatists. But in the making an edition of a man of genius's work for libraries and collections, and such I conceive a complete edition of Dryden to be, I must give my author as I find him, and will not tear out the page, even to get rid of the blot, little as I like it. Are not the pages of Swift, and even of Pope, larded with indecency, and often of the most disgusting kind, and do we not see them upon all shelves and dressing-tables, and in all boudoirs ? Is not Prior the most indecent of tale tellers, not even excepting La Fontaine, and how often do we see his works in female hands ? In fact, it is not passages of ludicrous indelicacy that corrupt the manners of a people — it is the sonnets which a prurient genius like Master Little sings *virginibus puerisque* — it is the sentimental slang, half lewd, half methodistic, that debauches the understanding, inflames the sleeping passions, and prepares the reader to give way as soon as a tempter appears.

Wordsworth himself hastened to write his approbation of Scott's undertaking; he was not personally fond of Dryden but he appreciated his greatness and the importance of putting his complete works before a thoughtful public.

With such encouragement for the most ambitious of his literary plans Scott could not doubt that he would make of his printing business a profitable enterprise. With boyish zeal he entered into plans for enlarged business quarters. If the landlord won't come to terms, we'll build, he cried.

Life seemed such a gay adventure that he was ready for Herculean schemes. Everything he touched had

SIR WALTER SCOTT
*From a painting by Sir J. Watson Gordon*

been successful so far — the public applauded his verses, he could command unheard of prices for anything he would write or edit. Swift was to follow Dryden; there were innumerable projects ahead. He could do an enormous amount of work just because he did vary it; editing was a relief from poetizing; besides, if he made the intervals between his poetical romances longer he would the better whet the public appetite and prevent its becoming jaded. His labors as sheriff and clerk he had always been able to clean up with swift competence; he did not find them a burden, and they did give a basic income. At least the sheriffdom did; the clerkship was still vain labor as far as finances went, since he possessed merely its reversion. Eventually the incumbent would die, or be otherwise provided for, and then he would have a really adequate income. However, if this printing business went well he could be independent of these offices as he was already independent of private practice at the bar, and he would have more time for his writing and his family.

Before he was thirty-five he had four children: Sophia, born in 1799, Walter in 1801, Anne in 1803, and Charles in 1805. The responsibility of a family, however much it stimulated him toward increased effort, in no way aged his youthful spirits. Indeed, the constant presence of active unrepressed children increased his own love of noisy fun.

"Really, Scott," Charlotte would protest as she laughed at his frolics with them, "you are nothing but a child yourself!"

It was quite true. He regarded his children as com-

panions from the moment when they could sit astride a
pony and refrain from whimpering if they were thrown,
or grew weary. As soon as they could spring up from a
tumble without wasting time on bruises, vault the pony
and be off at top speed again, he took them off with him
on harum-scarum excursions. They learned to plunge
through the Tweed in calm waters and in the swollen
waters of storm; they learned to scramble up thorny
banks, to ride down steep inclines. They would stop
for hilarious picnics, boisterous games.

They were rarely hushed within doors or without.
Their father did not expect them to speak more softly
than he did himself; and he loved to roar. He greeted
the day's first arrival at his study with a shout, sending
him off to make the halls echo with taunts at the lazy-
bones, and good-natured clarion calls to breakfast. Re-
calcitrants often woke to find themselves doused with
cold water. Horseplay was the common form of humor
in the household, encouraged by a father who throve on
racket.

He had never wanted to repress their high spirits.
Rather did he egg them on to wilder fun. Not even his
study was sacred from their roistering. They piled in
whenever they chose; they rushed in with violent quarrel-
ling; they entered not much more decorously with some
new plan for merriment. There were, occasionally,
tangles in history or mathematics or Latin to be straightened out. The governess had been chosen by Scott more
for her good character and sturdy principles than for her
learning. In time the boys could, whenever the family

was in town, attend the Edinburgh High School. He could start their Latin himself, though his Latinity was naught to boast of, and he had, alas, no Greek at all. At any rate he was violently opposed to boarding school. Why should he deprive himself of his children just when they became interesting to him ? He argued that the best influence was that of the home. He could himself implant in his sons the virtues of honesty, endurance, and persistence which were the backbone of conduct, of morality. Charlotte could teach the girls feminine accomplishments perfectly well; he himself could do more for them than any school or governess by keeping them with him, especially outdoors.

He didn't think overmuch of modern education, or of these new-fangled books for children. There might be something in this new scientific interest; but there could be no sense in sugar-coating its findings before they were fairly verified, and feeding them to infants. For his part he believed in imaginative literature for children. He had thriven on it himself; he knew its worth by what it had done for him. He loved to see in his children's hands the romantic books he had dreamt over in his own childhood, a childhood far different from theirs. He had not then had abundant health; he had been a sickly little lame boy, who had lost the use of his leg before he was two years old. He thought he remembered how he finally learned to walk again, he the darling of his grandfather's household. He had at first crawled after the sheep; his canny grandfather had planned on his making the effort if he were left fre-

quently enough out in the beautiful Scotch fields with
the sheep. His pony had been but a midget, hardly bigger than a dog. He had had to have things in miniature
then. What a spoiled child he had been ! He smiled
as he remembered a thousand indulgences. His grandparents, his aunt, the servants of house and farm had all
made him their god. He had ruled his little kingdom
triumphant for years. He had been utterly unused to
children. When, later, he returned to Edinburgh and a
houseful of brothers and sisters, his mother had been his
refuge; so long as he could cling to her skirts he had
been happy. She would yield to his entreaties and sing
him old ballads, tell him old tales. His memory had
always been keen; he would astonish her by repeating
flawlessly everything that she told him; how she had
enjoyed displaying her prodigy to her friends ! He had,
he feared, been a bit of a prig.

His children were not precocious; they had not had to
substitute books for play. It had been years before his
health had ceased to be a matter of concern; at the age
his children were scrambling mountains, boating, riding,
shooting, he was more often than not confined to his
bed. His enormous strength had been a late develop-
ment. Yet the years of invalidism had not been barren;
the steady reading had stored his mind with stories which
he now retold to his children. His reading had led into
the antiquarian field which now stood him in such good
stead in his writing. He had not yet thought of novels;
he was busy with poetry. But he taught his children
history in the fascinating mode of story-telling. They

imbibed history and geography in the pleasantest sugar-
coated way; their father's stories were always vividly
true, alive with brave men, lovely ladies, gallant princes,
dashing soldiery. Their mother could tell them tales
of French revolution, of flight, of danger. But her
stories were those of her own experiences; they became
familiar with repetition. Their father, on the other
hand, wove his romances imaginatively; and his were
ever new. They could never predict in advance whether
he would carry them to the Highlands or march them
along the border; whether his tale would deal with
the clash of Highland clans, or with the bold raidings
of their own ancestor, the intrepid Border chieftain who
replenished his vanishing herds by the simple device of
stepping over the border to "lift" those of some less canny
Englishman. Their mother was almost always in the
audience of a rainy day when they hugged the fireplace;
as ready as any of them with a gay laugh of appreciation.
She was less ready to join the mad romps within doors
with which their father varied the monotony of stormy
weather. He sank the parent in the playmate within
and without. His children had no notion that they
should be seen and not heard; they were never told that
their father was busy and not to be interrupted. They
never were banished to the nursery; they played all about
the house; and they shared their parents' meals, where
they took it as a matter of course that the conversation
was always kept on their level.

Sunday was ever a day apart. Ashestiel was too far
from any town to make church-going easily possible espe-

cially as Scott preferred the horses to have a day of rest.
All week they were ridden or driven steadily; they, too,
needed a day to themselves. But though they might not
ride, the family were not deprived of exercise, or of
amusement. Even the morning's religious services were
interesting since Scott himself read aloud from the Bible,
preferably from the Old Testament, reading with the
same sense for dramatic interpretation with which he
read a ballad. He selected his readings, moreover, with
an eye for a story. Then, the readings over, the children rounded up the pack of dogs from their mother's
petted spaniel to their father's fleet greyhounds, with a
motley array of terriers and collies, children, parents,
dogs, and visitors making a gipsy cavalcade with servants bringing up in the rear with enormous baskets of
provisions. When the boys grew older, they undertook
the piloting of the baskets themselves. Charlotte saw to
it that the contents were sufficiently satisfying. She liked
her Scott to have the food he appreciated so thoroughly.
He was fond of telling his children about his father's
asceticism, the opposite of his own frank pleasure in food.
He loved to recount the tale of the soup he had praised
boyishly.

"Ay, but the soup's good," he had said.

"Good ?" his father had queried. "Good ?" He
lifted a spoonful to taste it critically. "Ay, bairns," looking sternly at his greedy sons, "too good." And the old
man with grave ostentation emptied his tumbler of water
into the good hot soup.

Walter Scott set his children no such example. He

enjoyed his food and liked them to follow with hearty appetite. These Sunday picnics were not meant to be chastening. They started with a long walk to some favorite spot far enough from the house to give the exercise that stirred up appetites, as well as to create a sense of remoteness from the affairs and places of every day. After the meal had been washed down with wine, well-diluted at the brook, while the larger dogs roamed through the woods, the lazier dogs settled down on the grass with the children. It was not long before the demand came for a story. Though he was a good listener, Scott was a better talker. As they passed through his mind stories took on character; he breathed into them sparks of his own tremendous vitality. On these Sunday picnics he drew his tales from the Old Testament, building up the details from his colorful imagination. These were tales from history even as his Scottish tales. He told them with the same gusto, the same boyish enthusiasm.

These were happy days. Friends came and went, new acquaintances were constantly being made; his reputation as a poet, essayist, and editor was already great and steadily growing; his mail was already filling up with petitions from less successful poets; boys were sending him their youthful effusions from schools and universities. With all kindliness he would answer each request, giving criticism of the gentlest, suggesting, emending, hunting out ways to help those less fortunate than he. With an active interest in a press he would, he felt sure, be better able to help struggling writers. He could put their works before the public and make their merits known.

Certainly he was already what some people called great, and he was on the road to riches. When, after years of undistinguished wifehood, Williamina died in 1810, he had won a large measure of fame for a man not yet forty, and was living in a style which even she could not have despised. He was still leasing Ashestiel for his country estate, but he was looking about for a farm in the neighborhood on which he would erect a house exactly to his liking, one with a conservatory with a fountain in the centre of it; and the house should be set right in the garden.

He already owned a house in town, easily worth ten thousand pounds; and his library, his dearest hobby, was worth much more than that. No poor struggling lawyer was he now, but a famous poet, who could command guineas in the thousands for anything that he cared to write or to edit. Would he have been so bad a match for Williamina? But she had been false; and his Charlotte had been true. A dear companion she had been; perhaps their love hadn't been quite so glowing; but it had stood the test of time. They were fonder than ever of each other now; they were companions in the best sense. Charlotte walked by his side, she listened with admiration to everything he wrote; she loved to copy his verses in her own pretty hand. She was a ready listener to his every thought, his every plan. When he had recently been driving near Lasswade he had been unable to resist the sentimental impulse to see the cottage where they had spent their first summers; he decoyed the friend with him down the road, and sighed when he saw again the willow trees joined by the cross he had made, to make an arch for Charlotte over the gate. He grew garrulous. How happy they had been in that simple cottage ! How happy they were now in Edinburgh and at Ashestiel ! How happy they were going to be in this new house he would build ! Perhaps he hadn't been much as a lawyer; but no one could really dispute the power of his pen. Charlotte had been the first to predict his success; he was on the road to what she had first called him, "a great rich man."

# CHAPTER III

*Making butterflies that he [Jeffrey] may have the pleasure of pulling their legs and wings off.*

*People may say this and that of the pleasure of fame or of profit as a motive of writing. I think the only pleasure is in the actual exertion and research, and I would no more write upon any other terms than I would hunt merely to dine upon hare-soup. At the same time, if credit and profit came unlooked for, I would no more quarrel with them than with the soup.*

—WALTER SCOTT.

# CHAPTER III

S COTT had the more energy for his business project
because he had ceased to contribute to the *Edinburgh Review,* the literary czar of the early nineteenth century. Byron sang what should have been its
epitaph in *English Bards and Scotch Reviewers;* nevertheless it continued to dominate every genteel drawingroom of England and Scotland for many a long year.
Francis Jeffrey, the editor who guided it for twenty-
eight years, was a thorn in the flesh of all poets, even those
who could write the prose for which his magazine paid
magnificently — ten to twenty-five guineas for sixteen
page articles worth two guineas in the open market of
literature. Constable, the owner of the magazine, had
learned early that generosity paid rich returns. By his
generosity he drew into the circle of contributors all the
brilliant writers of the day, among whom Scott was prominent from the moment of his success with *The Lay of the
Last Minstrel.*

Yet Jeffrey's reviews of current literature were hard
pills for authors to swallow. His was a caustic vein of
criticism dictated by a mind trained in legality. For, like
Scott, Jeffrey was a lawyer whose practice left him more
leisure than lawyers can thrive on. He could add to his
attendance at court the editorship of a magazine and the
authorship of numberless political and critical essays.

Byron reflected the bitterness of many an injured poet when, ascribing the man's birthplace to a sixteenth story garret, he played with the idea that Jeffrey was the re-incarnation of that terrible Judge Jeffreys whose cold-blooded sentences had spread and swollen in legend:

> Some think that Satan has resign'd his trust,
> And given the spirit to the world again,
> To sentence letters, as he sentenced men.
> With hand less mighty, but with heart as black,
> With voice as willing to decree the rack;
> Bred in the courts betimes, though all that law
> As yet hath taught him is to find a flaw;
>
> .    .    .    .    .    .    .    .
>
> Who knows, if chance his patrons should restore
> Back to the sway they forfeited before,
> His scribbling toils some recompense may meet,
> And raise this Daniel to the judgment-seat ?
> Let Jeffreys' shade indulge the pious hope,
> And greeting thus, present him with a rope:
> "Heir to my virtues ! man of equal mind !
> Skill'd to condemn as to traduce mankind,
> This cord receive, for thee reserved with care,
> To wield in judgment, and at length to wear."

Part of this prophecy came true; Jeffrey's Whig affilia-tions made him a judge and a lord, but he did not live to be hanged in spite of the boy poet's hopes. And his magazine flourished though Tory gentlemen sometimes kicked an offending copy down the front steps and in-dignant militarists stopped their subscriptions. Walter Scott thundered at it when its politics hurt his excessive patriotism, such thunder as he had muffled when Jeffrey slaughtered *Marmion*.

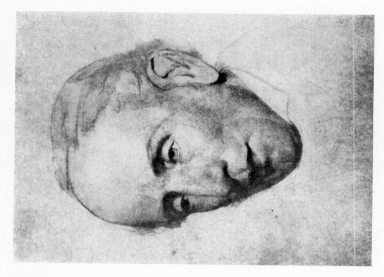

WILLIAM WORDSWORTH

*From a drawing by H. W. Pickersgill*

LORD BYRON

*From a painting by Thomas Phillips*

Slaughter it he did with an air of superiority, not tempering his language with the civility one might have expected toward a poet who was also a personal friend. His impartiality seemed to him praiseworthy until the appearance of his criticism in cold print only a few hours before dinner on a day when he was engaged to dine at the Scotts'. It was not that he chose to recant; but writers were an unduly sensitive lot; one never knew how they'd behave. Scott, now, seemed a normal man, hearty and healthy, a bluff genial lawyer, sheriff, country gentleman, unlike these pale poets of attenuated mind. Yet one never could tell. It would never do to dine with him tonight and quarrel with him tomorrow when the magazine would be out. He had best play safe.

He called the office boy and despatched him at once to Scott's Edinburgh house with this note and an advance copy of the *Review:*

DEAR SCOTT,

If I did not give you credit for more magnanimity than other of your irritable tribe, I should scarcely venture to put this into your hands. As it is, I do it with no little solicitude, and earnestly hope that it will make no difference in the friendship which has hitherto subsisted between us. I have spoken of your poem exactly as I think, and though I cannot reasonably suppose that you will be pleased with every thing I have said, it would mortify me very severely to believe I had given you pain. If you have any amity left for me, you will not delay very long to tell me so. In the meantime, I am very sincerely yours,

F. JEFFREY.

Scott had less trouble persuading himself than his wife of the obvious sincerity and friendliness of this letter.

Charlotte could not believe that anyone could speak ill of her husband; had not the whole world acclaimed him after the appearance of *The Lay of the Last Minstrel*? He was a great poet and Mr. Jeffrey was a very little man. He was jealous, you could take her word for it; jealous. Why he had had a better chance at law than her Scott; he had had the advantage of a year at Oxford; and he had not done nearly so well at the bar. Scott needn't protest; it was public property that his Whiggish sympathies had hampered him entirely; and he had done no better when he turned journalist and went to London. Everyone knew he half starved in London. He wouldn't ever have been editor of the *Review* either if Sydney Smith hadn't gone away and had to resign. Why was he made editor anyhow? He was such an ill-tempered little man all full of spite; he hardly ever had a good word to say of anyone. No one wrote poetry to suit him; why didn't he write some himself and show people how it should be done? Because he couldn't and he knew it; and that made him jealous. The little woman was thoroughly aroused. Her husband was altogether too good-natured, that he was. When Mr. Jeffrey came to dinner he always talked smartly; he was clever, yes, she wouldn't deny that. But no matter what person or poem or deed came into discussion he always had some fault to find. No one could talk better than he, except her Scott; that was half the trouble; he talked so cleverly and convincingly that he made one feel uncomfortable; when he was present nothing was quite right. All Scott's efforts to palliate, to qualify each fault-finding with a new bit of praise did not remove that feeling of wrongness when Jeffrey was there. He had better not come tonight; it would be easy to fill his place; who was in town that Scott would like to have ? or she could just shorten up the table; they could do very well without Mr. Jeffrey.

Scott would not have it; Jeffrey should come to dinner; he should not think that Scott's friendship depended upon false praise; for surely Charlotte could see that praise from Jeffrey would have to be false if this were what he really thought. Didn't she see that it was, after all, rather fine and courageous of him ? Of course it did sound ill-tempered; but let us hope it wasn't meant to be so. Didn't the note say that he had not meant to give pain ? That was pretty near an apology, wasn't it ? Anyhow think how foolish they'd look before their guests if Jeffrey weren't there. People would say they were petulant poets, a silly couple who couldn't have a man to dine unless he spoke well of their poetry. Charlotte smiled wanly at his inclusion of her. But she could not stand against him; she never had. If he insisted of course Jeffrey could come; oh yes, she'd be civil to him; she wouldn't insult a guest however much he had insulted *them*. Only she never could like him again.

She was quite civil; she answered him when he spoke to her with the extreme of calm politeness; but all through dinner she kept her eyes turned away from him as much as possible. In the drawingroom she contrived to be at a distance from him for the greater part of the evening. He had come because Scott had written him the friendli-

est of notes assuring him that the review — though he
hoped sincerely that neither booksellers nor public would
agree with it — had not in the least disturbed either his
digestion or his friendship for the critic. He greeted
Jeffrey with cordiality in which there was not the trace of
strain. Indeed the little man had quite forgotten that
he deserved not to have been well received when he came
up to Mrs. Scott to bid her good-night. As he bent over
to kiss her hand she said sadly, "Well, good-night, Mr.
Jeffrey. They tell me you have abused Scott in the *Review*. I hope Mr. Constable has paid *you* very well for
writing it."

Jeffrey was physically a great contrast to Scott whose
brawn made Jeffrey appear even smaller than he was.
Scarcely five feet tall, he was made in a delicate mold,
one who looked as if he were born to utter pleasant
nothings instead of hurling barbed darts of wit and irony.
But the look in his vivacious black eyes was constantly
contemptuous. He looked sharply at the world in order
to scorn it. And yet he could play the agreeable squire,
gossiping gaily with Jeannie Carlyle, finding mutual ancestors in their game of light flirting which Carlyle enjoyed almost as much as they. Jeffrey was somewhat of a
lady's man especially in his later years; he would single
out pretty women and witty women, kissing their hands,
bowing solicitously over them and uttering airy nothings.

Yet at the time when he slew *Marmion* he was not
interested in women or in much else. As Scott said he
had cultivated a stoical indifference, a stern repression of
enthusiasm that was death to any true appreciation of

poetry; and he might have added, of life. He was a
keen judge of the structure of a poem; he could decide
whether or not it were true to the canons of poetry;
but he could not go beyond this cool consideration. It
was quite true; Jeffrey had no enthusiasms, no zest for
poetry or life. He found in his bitter reviews, his sharp
speeches, a solace for the loneliness of his life. Perhaps
when Scott forgave him readily there lingered in his
mind the pathos of Jeffrey's letter to him when Mrs.
Jeffrey had died after four years of marriage:

> You do not know, my dear Scott, how entirely I had limited
> all my notions of earthly happiness to domestic society and
> affection, and how completely I had found it there without
> intermission or alloy. It was rather early to part with it,
> and just when fortune was beginning to smile upon us, and
> friends to increase in number and value.
>
> I cannot come soon to Ashestiel. That journey was almost
> the latest subject of my poor Kitty's solicitude, and she talked
> of it with delight and confidence almost as long as she was
> able to talk of anything. There is nothing indeed which
> melts and overcomes me so completely in the recollection of
> her illness as the unquenchable and unbroken hope with
> which she looked forward to her recovery and future en-
> joyments. . . She had so often been ill, indeed, and had al-
> ways recovered so rapidly that it scarcely entered into my
> imagination that there could be one illness of which she could
> not recover. . .
>
> I cannot force myself to leave my Kitty's grave at a dis-
> tance. I hope to be able to come to you by and by.

The tiny man had covered his grief by showing the
world all his accumulated bitterness, thinking, perhaps,
by his acerbity to enlarge his stature. When he wrote of
*Marmion* his loneliness was unalleviated; when, two

years later, he submitted to Scott, still his friend, the
proofs of his review of *The Lady of the Lake,* his heart
had softened.   This time he wrote:   "I am now sensible
that there were needless asperities in my review of *Marmion.*"  Scott's magnanimity had won the day, helped
by the mollifying influence of the American who later
became the second Mrs. Jeffrey.

Meanwhile in spite of the tremendous influence of the
*Edinburgh Review* Jeffrey's carping animadversions
failed to stem the tide of *Marmion's* triumphant progress;
*Marmion* was an instantaneous best seller.  The first
edition of two thousand, an expensive quarto, priced at
a guinea and a half, sold out in less than a month.  A
second edition of three thousand hardly lasted out the
season; six thousand sold the following year, five thousand the next, nine thousand the next, and so on year
after year.  Entering into the full glare of its popularity
*The Lady of the Lake* had no need of Jeffrey's plaudits;
it was taken to the public heart at once.  Earls and com-
moners christened their daughters Margaret in tribute
to The Lady.  Three plays were based upon it, and then
an opera. Walter Scott had waked to find himself
famous after the publication of *The Lay of the Last
Minstrel;* now not even the most carping of critics
could deny the freshness of his laurels.

Popular acclaim, however, was no longer intoxicating.
One could not continue to be thrilled.  What was thrill-
ing was his business acumen in having *The Lady of the
Lake* not only printed but published by a company of
his own; his would be the triple profits of poet, printer,

and publisher. He was no longer tied to Constable, that astute bookman who had known he was betting on a sure thing when he made what seemed an extraordinarily generous offer for *Marmion*. He let Jeffrey criticize how he would; though he owned the *Edinburgh Review,* he was not one to gag its editor. Jeffrey was never called upon to praise the books published by his employer; Constable published *Marmion;* Jeffrey damned it. Fortunately his criticism had been impotent to harm its sales.

With his faith in Scott's market value confirmed Constable was the more ready to yield to his insistence upon the merits of Ballantyne's Canongate Press. He turned over to Ballantyne more and more of his printing business. There was no suspicion in his mind that Scott was financially interested.

The fact of Scott's partnership had, as he directed, been kept secret. For one thing he loved secrecy; he seemed to get an exhilaration from hearing discussed freely in his presence affairs in which he was not known to be intimately concerned. Moreover he had always felt the romance of mystery. The deepest of his motives, however, was the wish to conceal his connection with "trade"; it was not genteel to be engaged in trade. From his childhood he had reverenced gentility. He had been almost from the cradle an ancestor worshipper; he had originally memorized and collected ballads for the mere joy of commemorating the exploits of the border chieftains, his grandfathers. These gay men, these bold riders, these chivalrous robbers were the stock of which he was sprung. No upstart he, but a gentleman, the son of gentlemen. When his mother was to visit him he wrote her solicitously; she must bring one of the servants to serve her as personal maid that she might travel "like a lady as you are."

So whereas he might engage in trade as a partner of Ballantyne, the transactions must be *sub rosa*. James Ballantyne proved as close-lipped as his benefactor. Scott's stiff-necked insistence upon the use of the Ballantyne press, though it was complained that the printing was too fine, the expense too great, excited no suspicious comment; Scott had always been such an enthusiastic befriender of lesser men that his protection was taken as merely the expression of friendship.

Constable, however, began to feel a certain irritation at Scott's complete reliance on James Ballantyne and later on his brother John. Constable was an astute fair-minded man, willing to humor a successful author, though for his own part he thought Scott permitted these tradesmen to be a bit too familiar. Maybe Ballantyne was as good a literary critic as Scott said he was; maybe he was as good a friend; one's friends needn't all be gentlemen. And Ballantyne was a good enough fellow. But hang it ! he was a tradesman; and what was the earthly use of Scott's consulting him all the time ? Why couldn't he just go ahead and get things done ? That big edition of Dryden had gone off well; why didn't he get Swift finished ? All this haggling and arguing with Ballantyne did no good; he, Constable, was the publisher; let Ballantyne stick to his presses.

JOHN BALLANTYNE
*From an original painting*

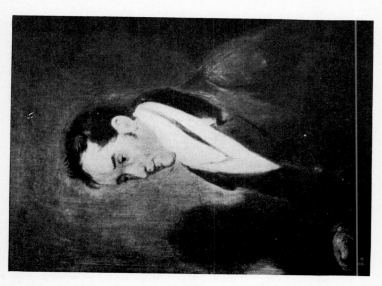

JAMES BALLANTYNE
*From the portrait at Abbotsford*

That is just what Ballantyne would not do. He was proud of Scott's friendship more than of his patronage; and he was somewhat jealous of Constable, Constable the successful, Constable the gentleman. He began to have grandiose notions; why shouldn't he turn bookseller and publisher and reap double profits? why should he be merely a printer? He poured out his ideas to Scott, finding him a willing listener just now when, for all his kind forbearance, he felt a human resentment against Jeffrey and Constable — after all Jeffrey was only the editor, Constable the owner of the *Review* which had been savage to *Marmion*.

And Ballantyne knew how to strike the right note, that of helping a friend in distress. John Ballantyne, his feckless younger brother, had arrived in town with a wife; and what was he to do with him? There wasn't any work he could do around the printing office except that little matter of bookkeeping. James wasn't much good at accounts himself; they took too much time, and he never could see the use of them. But Scott was always asking for an accounting of the business, always wanting to know how things stood financially. Now wouldn't it be a good idea to utilize John's real knowledge of figures? So John was installed as clerk at two hundred pounds a year. The clerkship, however, could hardly take all his time, much as the printing business had expanded. He could perfectly well set up as a bookseller in opposition to Constable, if he had a little backing: bookseller and publisher. *The Lady of the Lake* could be their first venture; anything of Scott's would be suc-

cessful enough to put a firm on its feet. It was hardly
conceit on Scott's part to recognize this obvious fact.
And for all his arguments with Charlotte and himself he
knew that Jeffrey's slurs rankled. He would like to
show him . . .

That, after all, was a mean motive. What he really
wanted was to relieve James's anxiety about John and
help that young man to his feet. The Ballantynes
weren't gentlemen in the accepted sense — Constable
needn't keep rubbing that in — but they had been schoolfellows for a short time, and he liked them. He didn't
care a fig if their father had kept a shop; it had been a
very pleasant shop. He had bought there the best top
he ever owned; and his aunt had always commended its
broadcloth. She always said Ballantyne was a good
judge of fabrics. James might have been a shopkeeper,
to be sure; he had been interested in printing nevertheless; and a very good printer he was, too.

John had, indeed, been another kettle of fish. He had
agreed readily enough to his father's plans of making
him a shopkeeper, but he had urged a season in London
first to learn how the shops there did business. And it
would do no harm if he learned accounting there; he was
good at figures as all the town knew; hadn't the school-
master praised him, again and again ? So though he
was but a young lad, his father sent him to London. He
was not too proud when he came back to Kelso to pick
up the tape measure and shears; down on his knees he
would go, whistling the latest air from the London stage,

to measure country bumpkins for breeches when they entered their country's service.

His vaunted skill in figures made a sorry mess of his father's affairs, however, when this gay young man was too sleepy after nights of gaiety to add up straight. He spent money faster than it came in; and before many years had reduced his father to poverty. The poor old man found a pitiful refuge with James in Edinburgh, being given a sinecure job in the printing office. John having enjoyed life thoroughly and run the whole gamut of delightful vices, married, and presented himself in Edinburgh in the appealing figure of repentant prodigal. What could James do but persuade Scott to permit him to add John to the staff and find an outlet for his energies in a business sure to succeed bountifully ? How could any publisher do aught but succeed when he carried the writings of the great Scott ?

And, by the way, what about that edition of Swift ? Was that definitely sold to Constable ? or could the new house have it ? After all, why shouldn't Scott be a partner in the concern that garnered wealth from his pen ? Constable had made a pretty sum out of him already. To be sure Constable had been fairly generous, but not as generous as others would be. James reminded Scott of his having insisted that he did not want Constable or anyone to look upon him as a monopoly, of his having compared publishers to farmers who "thrive best at a high rent" using their best effort to sell books which have cost them dear. The new publishing house could pay him a larger sum down than ever Constable had; and in addition Scott could figure on part of those profits which now were all Constable's.

James Ballantyne had a persuasive voice, rich, deep, and melodious. Its music was so pleasant that its logic seemed truth. As he talked he pulled at his thick black beard, in his earnestness screwing his handsome face up into fantastic grimaces. He jerked his sentences less than his features, but sometimes these, too, went forward in hops as his upper lip twisted itself scornfully toward his nose. A good man, James, sound of sense, solid in judgment, reflected Scott, and a pleasant companion, too. He mightn't be a gentleman in the social register, but there was no kinder fellow; and he certainly burned incense with a generous hand. Maybe he was right. Maybe this was the time to start things for himself. Constable's partner, Hunter, had been plaguey rude of late. How he did detest that fellow !

Still, was John Ballantyne the person to oversee the enterprise; did James think he really would settle down and behave himself ? After all, he hadn't exactly acquitted himself with credit in Kelso, either as a man or as a bookkeeper (he refrained from saying tailor, not wishing to offend James). But James was sure John was turning over a new leaf; he was a married man now with all the follies of youth behind him. He was a clever lad, no one could deny. If he put his mind to it he would make a business hum.

John came to plead his own case. A little man with a high squeaky voice, he hopped about like an animated scarecrow. He saw everything from the humorous angle. Everything to him was a gay adventure; nothing was difficult; life itself was all a game. He was full of ardor about the new enterprise, ready with a thousand schemes, confident, happy, witty, and incorruptibly good-humored. Nothing offended him, neither references to his somewhat shady past nor doubts of his ability to carry out all that he proposed. He answered objections with puns, disarmed doubt with merry laughter. He made his companions so thoroughly good-natured and pleased with themselves that they inevitably became pleased with him, too, and believed him as capable as he pronounced himself.

They should have their publishing house, these two good brothers, and Scott would be a sleeping partner as he had been and continued to be in the printing house. He would keep them busy enough. Of course it would be handy to have that multi-volumed edition of Swift; was he really tied to Constable?

At any rate he wasn't going to stand any more of Hunter's carping; Hunter might be Constable's partner but he needn't try to bully him. Hunter's criticisms of the Swift were hardly in good taste; why didn't the fellow show more courtesy? Maybe he didn't believe in the undertaking; maybe he'd be glad to get out of it.

Self-persuaded, Scott sat down and wrote Constable that from Hunter's attitude he concluded that they were tired of the undertaking; they had probably committed themselves too hastily, and he would therefore be glad to cancel the agreement. Constable meditated over this

letter for some days.  There were rumors in town about
Scott's starting up a rival to the *Review;* maybe they were
not without foundation.  That might be what was back
of this proposal; Scott wanted his time for other schemes.
An irritable tribe, these authors.  But it wouldn't do to
lose without a struggle this profitable poet.

Constable's answer was a marvel of restraint; it was
composed as carefully as if it had been a literary master-
piece.  It began, "We are anxious to assure you that we
feel no dissatisfaction at any part of our bargain about
Swift."  The whole letter would have mollified anyone
who had not made up his mind beyond hope of change.
It was in no sense a release from the contract, rather a
statement of the firm's eagerness to see it through.

Scott had scarcely received it when he sat down and
penned a choleric reply, taking for granted that the contract was now broken by mutual consent.  Mr. Hunter
with his uncomplimentary tongue was the scapegoat.
Constable must be credited with enough good temper to
offset several partners since he showed no active resentment against the almost insulting conclusion to Scott's
letter which assumed that the only connection between
them was a business one to be settled in pounds and
pence:

In the present circumstances, I have only a parting favour
to request of your house, which is, that the portrait for which
I sat to Raeburn shall be considered as done at my debit, and
for myself.  It shall be of course forthcoming for the ful-
filment of any engagement you may have made about engraving, if such exits.  Sadler will now be soon out, when we
will have a settlement of our accounts.

Thus haughily did Scott write to the firm that had treated him well, while to others he wrote:

Constable, like many other folks who learn to undervalue the means by which they have risen, has behaved, or rather suffered his partner to behave very uncivilly towards me. But they may both live to know that they should not have kicked down the ladder till they were sure of their footing.

Constable might well have retorted that ladders are of little avail to men untrained in climbing; he contented himself with a courteous refusal of Scott's somewhat supercilious offer to take over the Raeburn portrait. Scott pronounced Constable an honest and enterprising man whose vanity overpowered his discretion. Constable had his own opinion of Scott's discretion, but he was too shrewd a business man not to believe that the breach, though complete to all seeming, might not eventually heal to their mutual advantage. He even got some amusement from Scott's hot letter stopping his subscription to the *Review:* "The Edinburgh Review *had* become such as to render it impossible for me to continue a contributor to it. — *Now,* it is such as I can no longer continue to receive or read it." Quite cheerfully Constable took his pen to cross out Scott's name from the list of subscribers with a 'STOPT ! ! !'

Scott began to feel that he ought to do something to protect the youth of the land from the false politics of the *Review;* it had altogether too much authority both literary and political, and when it was right in one field it was like to be wrong in the other. Young people ought to be guided better in both fields; and even older people were wrongly influenced by such a sheet. Jeffrey encountering Scott, and mindful of rumors, suggested that they make peace.

"I promise you, Scott, I have done with party politics in the *Review*."

"You have already committed yourself. The Whigs have you in the hollow of their hand; your paper is nothing but a party tool; and its influence, as I have often warned you, is bound to be hurt with fair-minded people. Now you will have to face the consequences."

"Consequences ? But there are but four men I fear as opponents." And Jeffrey smiled.

Scott was too thoroughly in earnest, too anxious to justify to himself the course to which he was now practically committed to be turned aside.

"Who are these?"

"Yourself for one," bowed Jeffrey.

"Certainly you pay me a great compliment," answered Scott smoothly. "Depend upon it I will endeavor to deserve it."

Quick to catch the undertone of irony Jeffrey snapped him up. "You would not join against me ?"

"I would indeed, if I saw proper opportunity: not against you personally, but against your politics."

"Sir, you are privileged to be violent."

For all their sparring Jeffrey and Scott parted friends and next day Jeffrey dined with Scott hardly aware of the bomb Scott was preparing to explode at his very feet.

"I owe Jeffrey a flap with a fox-tail on account of his review of *Marmion*," he wrote to his brother, "and thus doth 'the whirligig of time bring about my revenges.' "

It was not hard to unite with him others "whose reputations Jeffrey has murdered, and who are rising to cry wo upon him, like the ghosts in King Richard." The rival to the *Edinburgh Review,* the *Quarterly Review* was fast hatching. John Murray, the young London bookseller and publisher, had foreseen this as soon as Jeffrey's review of *Marmion* appeared. He reflected that Scott, the best seller of the day, would not be exactly pleased. The tone of the review was bound to hurt his susceptibilities as a gentleman. He had a feeling that as a result Scott's relationship with Constable who was, after all, the owner of the magazine Jeffrey edited in such cavalier fashion, would become strained. He might be able to help the strain into a fracture; and he might himself be standing conveniently by with a sling for the broken arm. One never knew with poets. Certainly Scott was a moneymaker for any publisher to covet. There could be no harm in sounding out the possibilities.

Murray gave the matter much thought, wondering how to approach the great man. Finally he decided to sound out Ballantyne. It was common knowledge that Scott was hand in glove with him; that he would permit no one else to print his books. It was said that he took the man's advice in all matters.

It was obvious, anyhow, that if he wanted a close connection with Scott he would have to have one with Ballantyne. The simplest method was to arrange for him to print various undertakings; and he forthwith wrote, suggesting various schemes which necessitated a personal interview.  At this time Murray was a fairly successful young man, a London bookseller of good reputation but by no means on a par with the powerful Constable of Edinburgh.  He had already had a slight finger in Scott's pie, having been a sharer in *Marmion*.  Constable, having disgorged so large a sum for the poem, adopted the very common custom of the time, of letting two or three minor booksellers join him in the publishing project, each paying part of the costs and receiving a part of the profits.  Murray was the London bookman chosen.  He had therefore had a foretaste of the prosperity Scott's literary efforts brought to those connected with him, and he desired a much closer and more exclusive connection.

Ballantyne was, naturally, pleased to have his press employed.  He himself suggested a meeting with Murray in Yorkshire.  The astute young bookseller was soon in possession of all Ballantyne's projects: he learned of the proposed new publishing house and offered himself at once as the London representative.  He learned of the intention of Scott to help Ballantyne publish an *Annual Register* which should counteract and undermine the influence of the *Edinburgh Review*.  The time was ripe to see the great man himself and make a bargain on his own account.

Scott was easily approachable.  All the world was welcome at Ashestiel whither Murray, upon his request for an interview, was immediately invited.  Between them they concocted the *Quarterly Review* which Scott agreed to feed and to coddle though he could not see his way to undertake the editorship. Murray did not urge him, having learned from Ballantyne that Scott was at work not only upon Swift, and a new poem, but also a novel, a Scotch novel which honest James pronounced as fine as the poems. These were prizes which with care, Murray thought, might fall into his hand. Meantime there was the *Quarterly* to arrange. Scott was confident that they could count upon all his literary friends, indeed, upon most of the brilliant writers of the day, for whom had the *Review* not insulted ? Certainly no good Tory, like himself, would stand for any more of its Whiggish nonsense.

For editor they finally settled upon William Gifford, an able man, though one who needed guidance, which Scott would be pleased to give. He forthwith wrote Gifford an encyclopædic letter outlining the privileges and duties of the editorship, laying out a platform and an ideal. Gifford was a little man, so huddled upon himself that he seemed to have been squashed. His two sides seemed not to belong together so ill did they match. To make matters worse, one eye was hardly an eye at all. He was rarely without a racking cough, and from time to time he fell heir to every disease known to doctors. Yet in spite of his ill health, to which it was charity to ascribe his literary indolence, he was a likable chap with recognized ability. Properly spurred by Scott and the other authors who would rally to their standard, Gifford might be trusted to turn out excellent criticism and manage a well-rounded magazine. He had wide learning, he was extremely well informed, he was clever and witty and reliable. His wit was, indeed, at times a bit too sharp, but he could be kept in hand.

The *Quarterly* which was to be "so savage and tar- tarly," that was to review Scott's yet unborn novels suit- ably, since under cover of anonymity he could and did review them himself, was hatched with enthusiasm. Scott poured out his eagerness for the scheme to such friends as he hoped to interest in it, urging secrecy that the magazine might burst upon Jeffrey and Constable with complete and devastating surprise. Yet at no time did he cease to be friendly with either Jeffrey or Con- stable. He did, however, gloat over the thought of Con- stable's discomfiture when not only the *Quarterly* but the *Annual Register* he and James Ballantyne were fathering, should appear to contest the field with the *Edinburgh Review*. And then Constable would also have to face the direct rivalry of John Ballantyne set up as bookseller and publisher in Edinburgh, his capital being only his own merry self, the necessary financial backing furnished by Scott, though Constable was not to know this. And the new firm would be lodged in attractive quarters, such as gentlemen would appreciate, quite different from Constable's dingy place of business.

Scott's own definition of his attitude toward the world was this: "The feeling was born with me not to brook a disparaging look from an emperor, when I had the least means of requiting it in kind, and I have only to hope it is combined with the anxious wish never to de- serve one were it from a beggar."

Constable was no emperor, Jeffrey was, indeed, a

friend — maybe Charlotte was right, and his disparagements proceeded from jealousy. Anyhow he would be independent of them both. From now on he was the arbiter of his own destiny; poet, printer, publisher. Only a few would know the full circle of his activities; his secret would be kept. But Constable would know that it was Scott's patronage that made his rivals prosper: John Ballantyne and Company, booksellers and publishers; James Ballantyne's *Annual Register;* the *Quarterly Review.* The house of Constable had best look to its foundations; the house of Scott was rising with a foundation of rock. Walter Scott, poet, perhaps novelist; Walter Scott, great rich man.

# CHAPTER IV

*Author as I am, I wish these good people would recollect that I began with being a gentleman, and don't mean to give up the character.*

—WALTER SCOTT.

## CHAPTER IV

IT WAS proper for a successful man to plan out an estate for himself, one which he could leave to his children; his son should not be plain Walter Scott, but Walter Scott of Abbotsford. The land which he had bought within his sheriffdom was the site of an old abbey near a ford on the Tweed; it was about five miles down the river from Ashestiel. At present it was bare of beauty, being a tangle of neglected furze. All this he would change; he would create a symphony of woods and lawns and gardens and then he would place in them a dwelling-house fit for his Charlotte. The original plans were less magnificent for the house than for the grounds, but Charlotte good-naturedly consented to occupy for the present the existing farmhouse so that they might live in their domain and finally settle upon the exact type of residence suited to them and its surroundings.

The farmhouse was not commodious, but it could be made to do though there was but one small sittingroom where Scott could have privacy at his desk only by drawing a curtain about himself. However this did not greatly disturb him, since he had formed the habit of working while the household slept. He liked to keep up a fiction of his being a lazy indolent man, whose time was his own for whatever pursuits he chose: hunting, fishing, riding, walking, talking. His legal offices kept him busy a few hours a day six months in the year; occasionally he was kept fully occupied by some committee, such as that concerned with the reform of Scotch jurisprudence of which he was secretary. For the rest he liked to be thought a gentleman of complete leisure. To this end he acquired the habit of rising at five in the morning, and at six was at his desk, having in the hour's time performed a meticulous toilet — he had no sympathy for dressing-gown and slippers as the poet's garb — and visited the stables. He moved about surrounded by all sorts of dogs to whom he talked as if they were humans. As many as liked returned with him to his study where howsoever chill the day he kept a window open for their egress and ingress. He wrote steadily and rapidly so that at nine, when he breakfasted with his family, he had a tidy packet of manuscript ready to send off to James Ballantyne's presses. He rarely revised and his memory was too exact to make it necessary for him to keep the manuscript by him. Quite early it became his custom to have his first sheets go to press while he was in the act of composition, though he never knew exactly what was going to happen next in poem or tale. Plots and characters formed themselves as he wrote, his memory serving up for his use enormous stores of anecdote, scene, and dialogue. Occasionally he went back to his desk for an hour or two after breakfast, though when guests were in the house he preferred to turn at once to their entertainment.

For a time in 1812 he did not write at all, being com-

ABBOTSFORD

*From a painting by J. M. W. Turner*

ABBOTSFORD IN 1812

*From an engraving by W. Richardson*

pletely absorbed in the removal in May to Abbotsford, and in the aggrandizement of his new estate. Twenty-four cartloads of furniture wended their way, a procession attended by a string of delighted and curious bare-footed boys and girls, all the countryside gaping at the Sheriff's belongings. Behind straggled live stock of every conceivable kind, from the children's pets to the pigs and cows. There were mettlesome riding horses, and heavy farm horses. There were the children's ponies and Charlotte's matched carriage horses. There were fleet greyhounds and overfed spaniels; huge turkeys and diminutive bantams. But public curiosity and mirth overflowed at the wagonloads of armor, lances, swords, bows, targets, helmets, banners, bugles, and muskets. The bestowal of all this gear in the limited space of the existing farmhouse at Abbotsford required careful adjustment. It occupied space sadly needed for living quarters, but Charlotte made no difficulties, though she did make mild fun of the mess of old guns and coins with which her dresses and bonnets had to consort.

Scott did not mind the comparatively small inelegant house because he knew that the world knew that such an arrangement was purely temporary, dictated not by economy or necessity, but by his desire to erect a truly grand domicile. So long as no one thought him in straitened circumstances he was content to work out first his schemes for the landscaping of the grounds. The present hundred and twenty acres were but a tenth of the estate he would soon possess; his would be no modest park, but an elegant landed estate. Almost at once he bought a hill and some woods, and began to figure upon that mile along the Tweed which he would in time acquire. He threw himself wholeheartedly into the planning and planting of his acres, gloating over the fair woods and pleasant prospects that would be theirs in a few years. He started his occupancy of his own estate with a grand revel, every workman for miles about dancing and eating and drinking on his green until dawn. When the house should be built there would be a grander feast, for gentry as well as peasantry.

He was a comparatively young man, barely in his forties; he owned Abbotsford and had a thousand pounds in his pocket. The holder of his clerkship, indeed, had so far refused to die; but the government had at last stepped in with a pension for him so that the income could now come into Scott's pockets, thirteen hundred pounds a year. As sheriff he received three hundred, his wife had two hundred a year from her brother; there were eighteen hundred already. With his writings he now could count on a full twenty-one hundred pounds a year, putting his earnings with his pen at a modest sum. He could dig much more gold up from this inexhaustible mine of his. So long as the public would read he would write.

When Charlotte had married him he had been unable to duplicate her little income; now that was but a penny in his grand total. He might well plan on a great estate; he could well afford it. If he had previously made enormous sums from his poetry under Constable's manage-

ment he would make perhaps double the amount now
that he had a share in the publishing profits too. It was
with pride that he told Charlotte she need not curb her
expenses in any way; she might gratify any of her wishes.
He himself bought with unrestrained zeal collections of
old armor, of old books. They lived surrounded with
ponies for the children, fine horses for himself (he liked
to remember that he wrote *The Lay of the Last Minstrel* because he wanted a new horse for his manœuvres
in the volunteer cavalry), a carriage for Charlotte, dogs
for every member of the household, peacocks, butlers,
coachmen, servitors for every purpose. He was a laird,
a patriarch, living richly in his rich domain. The house
that would rise must be one fitting for a man of wealth
and a man of fame.

Without vanity he recognized that he was the most
widely read poet of his day. Until *Childe Harold* de-
veloped a change in literary taste, any poetical feast of
Scott's contrivance was swallowed by a greedy public in
two bites. The morning when Byron woke to find himself famous was — though he did not immediately recognize it — the hour of Scott's swansong as a poet. He
thought himself modest in taking from the new firm
only two thousand pounds for his unwritten *Rokeby*
after their first venture with his poetry had been such a
magnificent success: *The Lady of the Lake* sold twenty
thousand copies in a few months. It was common gossip that the poem had put money in the pockets of half
Scotland; had not the price of post-chaises been raised

because of the rush of tourists to see his Lady's lake ? He had benefited the whole countryside. *Rokeby* would do as well.

He was right to plan a bigger house than he had at first intended. Charlotte should have a mansion as befitted her. At Ashestiel he had often squeezed in a total of thirty-two, family and guests, though the house had been intended for but ten. Here in the farmhouse, only the merest handfuls could be put up; in the new house they would really have room. Besides the friends, there were always the curious, some of whom to be sure were bores, but some of whom often proved interesting. His acquaintance was now so wide that there was always a fringe of the helpless, writers who needed alms, and actors who needed praise. All the great actors, too, were now his friends and admirers. Closest to him of them all was Daniel Terry, a young and successful comedian whose hero-worship of Scott was as whole-hearted as it was amusing. Though he was a little fellow, he made the most of his height, and attempted to carry himself like the huge man he adored. An Englishman, he conscientiously cultivated a Scotch burr so that his enunciation as well as his intonation might resemble that of his hero. He copied the trick of the lifted eyebrow and even was known to have walked with a limp, so far did his idolatry carry him. He modelled his handwriting so carefully on that of his hero that Scott humorously remarked that all he could say of any document would be that either he or Terry had written it.

Such adulation was not unpleasant. Moreover Scott

knew personally and was treated in friendly fashion by all the literary lights of the time; he corresponded with and visited Wordsworth and Southey; Byron wrote to tell him of the praises royalty had spoken of Scott; all the writing ladies to whom their generation accredited genius leaned on his approbation. He was a celebrity not alone in Edinburgh but in London itself. And he had achieved both reputation and wealth in the easiest possible way; he had merely amused himself writing verses. From childhood he had been interested in antiquarian lore, in the tales of his ancestors. It had been amusement to delve into the past, remembering as he collected dusty armor that live men had inhabited it. Flesh and blood ladies had worn those elaborate gowns; firm hands had held those lances. The past had never been dry and dust history to him; it was alive with gallant fighter and sheep stealer, fair lover and modest maiden. As he rode about hunting or supervising, even as he travelled to court in legal gown, he thought out his rhymes, so that he needed no great stretches of quiet hours, no deep seclusion in which to put them down on paper. Writing poetry for him was the mere transmission to paper of lines that jingled in his head.

Life was a gay affair. Here he was forty, proprietor of what would be a vast estate; his descendants would be proud of their ancestral acres; they would say: "Walter Scott knew what he was about when he planted this land. We have tried to keep things as he had them; he was a man with a vision of the future." His children would praise his forethought, his good taste; and his children's children would echo those praises. They would say, "His inheritance was not much; and his wife brought him only two hundred a year; but he bought and planted this vast estate. He made himself a great rich man."

The plaudits of the future were even sweeter to his ears than those of the present. He was a happy man. At his side was his admiring wife, companion of all his thoughts and dreams, ready to second any scheme he propounded, sure of his essential rightness in all things. The children were promising and for the present attractive. Except for the minor ills of childhood they were healthy young animals. Walter yawned over his Latin, to be sure, but then so did his father-tutor. Fortunately a lame duck of a clergyman turned up in time to undertake the task of drilling the boys properly so that they need not continue under the indifferent instruction of their father; he could at one step relieve the distress of a worthy scholar and the Latinity of a worthy parent, himself.

Meanwhile he had a satisfactory amanuensis acquired in the same philanthropic way. A young German whose literary schemes the new house of Ballantyne was publishing needed succor; the many-volumed edition of Swift was equally in need. Weber was set to work. In befriending him Scott was satisfying once more the paternalistic streak in his own nature. Weber was inclined to be a slave to the bottle; under Scott's watchful eye and that of Mrs. Scott, since he dined frequently at Abbotsford, this inebriety would be conquered. All went well for some time, when one afternoon as he and Scott were quietly working in the library .Weber drew two pistols and demanded instant satisfaction for some fancied insult. Scott's healthy body knew no nerves. He calmly pocketed both pistols, assuring the demented youth that nothing would give him more pleasure, but after all they must not alarm the ladies. They would eat dinner in pretended amity and then — the garden. The dinner went off smoothly until the end when Scott attempted to regulate Weber's potations. By that time an attendant, sent for secretly by Scott, arrived to take the unhappy youth in charge. All was well; but the edition of Swift was delayed.

It was not until 1814 that it was finally issued. The years since its undertaking had curiously gone full circle so that it was actually brought out by Constable for whose hands it had been originally intended and from whose hands it had been wrested. Many things had tended to bring about the complete reconciliation of author and publisher, not the least of them being the imperturbable friendliness of Constable. The irascible Mr. Hunter had died in 1812 so that Scott could deceive himself into thinking that his wrath had never been directed at anyone else in the firm, and that his application to Constable would not lower his pride. Of course Constable did not know that Scott was the firm of John Ballantyne and Company, at least the money side of it. Presumably the "and Company" was James Ballantyne. Breaking into a new business had proved less of a lark than John had thought; here he was about to publish *The Lady of the Lake* and he hadn't the faintest idea of how to go about it. How

many copies should he bind up for the first edition ?
How did one sell an edition anyhow ?   What steps had
to be taken to place a book on the market and put it
before the public ?   These were details of which John
was as ignorant as Scott.   There was nothing to do,
Scott felt, but for John to ask Constable for advice.   It
speaks well for Constable that at this time, immediately
after the breach, he should have been willing to help one
who had taken from him his best-selling author and who
had set up as his direct rival.   Perhaps he felt that it
would be eventually for his own interest to have Scott's
popularity unharmed.   At all events he freely gave help.
But by the time Hunter had died it was more than advice
that the firm of John Ballantyne needed.

By this time commercial credit was made difficult by
the American war of 1812.   John Ballantyne found the
banks unwilling to supply money for his use on the mere
security of the poems Scott was going to write.   The
profits which had poured in from *The Lady of the Lake*
had been freely spent both by Scott and by the easy-going
Ballantynes.   Moreover other schemes had lost as much
as that had made.   Scott's lame ducks might be worthy
men; their literary labors were rarely profitable.   The
*Annual Register* was a fine magazine; but the balance
sheet showed a deficit of a thousand pounds a year.
*Rokeby,* Scott's new poem, would undoubtedly retrieve
their fortunes; but that was not yet ready.   Scott had a
fancy to hold it up until he had finished *The Bride of
Triermain* which he intended to publish anonymously.

The two should come out in the same week to the mystification of the critics (especially Jeffrey) and to the profit of Scott and the Ballantynes. Finally *Rokeby* was issued alone, to be followed by the anonymous poem in two months; other critics were puzzled or suspicious; but Jeffrey was on the high seas, off to marry his American bride.

Meanwhile James Ballantyne had convinced Scott of the necessity of applying to Constable for substantial aid. John was willing to give up the publishing business if Constable would make no other terms. Scott felt that his personal income was so great, especially with the prospect of a sum in hand over the final settlement of his father's estate, that such humiliation was hardly warranted. He became convinced of the necessity before many months. After all it was not personal humiliation; Constable would be dealing with the Ballantynes; and all that could be said was that Scott had not of his own weight been able to carry over a new publishing concern. It would not be known that he was actually a partner. So long as he got along without public exposure he was fairly content. It had been a very vexatious affair all through. John Ballantyne was apparently constitutionally unable to take the direct line of speech. He could not bring himself to state without circumlocution the actual disagreeable facts. As a bookkeeper he rivalled the negligence of his brother. Neither one of them could keep things decently in order. It was frightfully annoying even for a rich man to be constantly tapped for sums ranging from a few pounds to several hundred. "For heaven's sake," he cried with pardonable irritation, "treat me as a man, not as a milch cow !"

For John Ballantyne's procedure had been constantly to deny financial pressure and then to send to Scott post-haste for funds to pay immediate bills. Scott would be dining at a ducal castle or with guests at Abbotsford when a horse all foam would gallop into the yard and a hot red-faced boy would send in a letter. The guests would stare, Charlotte would look at him anxiously, he would have to excuse himself from table, and hastily enclose a banker's draft. At first he contented himself with mild remonstrances to John and to James Ballantyne, urging the inconvenience to himself and the semi-publicity. After a while as these requests, nay demands, followed him about on his visits to authors and dukes he waxed sarcastic, especially as neither brother found time to acknowledge the receipt of his remittances. He advised James to find a monied partner as he could not permanently face supplying a deficit of two hundred pounds a month for the printing concern; and John had better wind up the affairs of the publishing firm and go out of business. Meanwhile there was nothing to do but make peace with Constable. More than three thousand copies of *Rokeby* had sold the first two days, but for all that it failed to duplicate the wide success of *The Lady of the Lake*. Byron had turned public attention to different verse. *Rokeby* was lapped up at Oxford; it was talked of in the drawingrooms of the genteel; it was, for any normal poet, a huge success; but for Scott ten thou-

sand in three months was small. For all the demands of the business and of Abbotsford it was distinctly
inadequate. Scott told himself that Constable and his
new partner Cadell made a very good bargain when they
took over a share in *Rokeby* and in the literary dinosaurs
of the Ballantyne programme. Their two thousand
pounds was but a fraction of what they would make. So
he soothed his pride, putting his judgment to sleep.
Meanwhile he gave heed to Constable's advice; Constable said that his responses to John's appeals for
money were but driblets; what was needed was a guarantee of a good sum, say four thousand pounds. Then
John could wind up the business satisfactorily — there
really was not room in Edinburgh for two concerns.
Scott expressed to the brothers his desire to retire
from both their firms; James could find other ways of
managing his printing business, and John could become
an auctioneer as he desired. As for him, his head ached
and he longed to be free of all these importunities.
Nevertheless he racked his brain until he found a way to
give the guarantee. He wrote to his friend the Duke of
Buccleuch, asking him merely for form's sake to guarantee his own signature; his income and expectations were
such that what he asked was scarcely more than a for-
mality; he cheerfully, and not without pride, listed his
income, and mentioned his expectations, including the
offer which had just come to hand of the poet laureateship, good surely for three or four hundred pounds a
year. The Duke readily consented to the guarantee, but
demurred at the laureateship. Why should Scott harness

his muse and write birthday odes ? Honors he did not need, being loaded with them already; besides the laureateship had become something of a joke and a reproach.

With the Duke's pleasant willingness to fall in with his plans Scott became immediately cheered and optimistic; he had no desire to saddle himself with the laureateship. He would make the money more easily with rhymes not for royal birthdays; and he could in his magnificence turn the favor in a direction where it would be a godsend. After all he had two legal offices, richly rewarded; and his literary output had been exceedingly profitable. Like Byron he was independent of royal grants; they two were men of affairs and substance. But Southey, now, was a man dependent upon literature for a livelihood; he had tasted success, yet only of a moderate measure. To him the stipend would be as valuable as the recognition. It pleased Scott to think that by not burdening himself he could benefit a fellow-craftsman. And after all the stipend proved to be only half its reputed value.

It was precisely at this time of business burdens that Scott stumbled upon the opening pages of the novel which James Ballantyne had hinted to Murray about at the beginning of the publishing venture. This novel had been started, had even been picked up again after a time, but had been put aside because of the lack of enthusiasm shown by those who saw it, and by the greater ease of writing verses. Now Scott surveyed it with satisfaction. Here was a new vein to be tapped.

He finished *Waverley* with a rush, pausing in his headlong composition only to write two articles, to please Constable, for the supplement to the Encyclopædia Britannica, articles which paid him one hundred pounds apiece. The novel he was determined to publish anonymously. From time to time in the past he had published anonymous poems, some of them in the style of the early seventeenth century, deriving much amusement from his anonymity. He had never given up his desire to mystify Jeffrey completely; and just now Jeffrey had lessened the sale of his Swift by his biting comments on Swift's character.

John Ballantyne was commissioned to take the first volume of *Waverley* to Constable and make terms for the unknown author. Though the copy was in John's writing, Constable was not deceived. Without waiting to see the completing volumes of the tale he offered seven hundred pounds for the copyright, a generous sum considering the stagnant state of the novel market. But it was not enough for Scott who demanded a thousand pounds. John Ballantyne trotted between Scott and Constable, transmitting offers, refusals, and finally compromises. The terms, which proved very much to Scott's advantage, were for equal shares in all profits. Now all he needed to do was to complete the many-volumed story.

Once more he had gauged the public taste correctly; once more he had accurately estimated the state of the literary market. The days of lurid fiction were over; no one wanted a new series of ghostly mysteries. Why imitate them ? Healthy romance was something different, something new. The accuracy of his judgment was proved by the instant success of *Waverley* even though it made its appearance in the season usually considered dull — almost midsummer. The first edition of a thousand copies melted like snow; two thousand more came upon the bookstalls only to be snatched therefrom. Edition followed edition. The clean romance of history, the hearty vigor of masculine action made of this novel something absorbingly and vitally interesting. Here was no book for pale girls to weep over. This was meat for mature men and women.

The instant success of *Waverley* put him in fine fettle. Here he was embarked on the jolliest of adventures. He could, as it were, write poetry with one hand and novels with the other. If the public taste had turned definitely away from his style of verse to Byron's, then he could push the prose the faster. He could at one and the same time mystify the critics and fill his purse. If he could do a novel in a month, then fortune would smile on him as never before. The summer evenings of three weeks, during which his mornings had been spent as clerk in court, had sufficed him for the major part of *Waverley*. Here was the best of larks.

And here lay the solution of the difficulties of John Ballantyne and Company. Light-hearted John had turned auctioneer, skipping over to France to buy baubles for society to covet. His bookseller's quarters were filled with unsalable stock, literary fossils representing golden guineas of Scott's outlay. To get rid of these required canny dealings. Constable was the predestined victim.

As each novel was offered to him, hard terms were made: to get the publishing of this novel he must agree to take over five thousand of John's useless volumes.

John suggested blithely that the new edition of *Waverley* for which there was speedily a demand, be given to whichever publisher made the highest bid. John's idea of a contract was vague; he apparently did not consider a contract binding if it did not conduce to one's greatest profits.

"My dear John," said Scott drily, "your expedients are all wretched. I never will give Constable, or any one, room to say that I have broken my word with him in the slightest degree. If I lose everything else, I will at least keep my honour unblemished; and I do hold myself bound in honour to offer him a *Waverley,* while he shall continue to comply with the conditions annexed."

The conditions, of course, were the purchase of dead stock from John Ballantyne and Company. If Murray and Blackwood would make handsomer offers on these various literary fossils, they might have the new novels. Constable had no lien on them.

John complained that Scott by his absurd scruples was hampering him. *He* hadn't made a fortune out of this publishing business; the profits hadn't exactly rolled into *his* pockets.

Scott retorted that John, when he boasted of having got nothing from the business, reminded him of the crane in the fable. "You may thank God," he snapped, "that it did not bite your head off. Would to God I were at let-a-be

for let-a-be." It was small comfort to reflect that John
had done his best. And now he must do his best to un-
coil the mischief John had made.

He permitted John to pit Longman against Murray in
the sale of *Guy Mannering,* only stipulating, when Longman took up the terms of fifteen hundred pounds down,
and the purchase of five hundred pounds' worth of John
Ballantyne's stock, that Constable be given a share in the
venture. Poor Constable had been inclined to balk at
the hard terms made by John; this device of keeping him
in the dark about *Guy Mannering* until he was offered
a minor share by Longman taught him a lesson. After
this he would not be likely to refuse any terms John
might propose. And Constable fell into the net prepared for him. So anxious was he to remain the publisher of Scott's novels, so completely convinced was he
of their commercial value, that he yielded to the
astute manœuvres of John Ballantyne (secretly directed
by Scott) and swallowed in one gulp the whole remain-
ing bulk of John Ballantyne and Company's literary
junk. John led him to believe that these were the terms
on which Murray and Blackwood would take the tales.
Constable had shown a tendency toward independence;
he had actually given printing to other men than James
Ballantyne. He must be taught his place.

Certainly he was ground between the two, Scott and
John Ballantyne. And his losses on these worthless volumes — such things as the madman Weber's valueless
edition of Beaumont and Fletcher fathered by Scott to
help a poor devil — mounted into thousands of pounds.

John Ballantyne, though now neither printer nor publisher nor bookseller, continued to draw a pretty profit from Scott's publications, being given a third of Constable's profits in return for his services as go-between. And yet such services were unnecessary since Constable had to know of the true authorship of the novels. Scott however, felt a certain reluctance to the actual performance of the canny bargaining; he still kept up the fiction that the business had been Ballantyne's; and that he had acted merely as friend and adviser. So between them they unloaded their stock and felt proud of their sharp dealing.

These were rich years for them all. Scott bought more and more land, not satisfied even with a thousand acres. He planned and planted, continually adding to his house where he entertained all the world. Rich men came with butlers and valets, poor men with hungry stomachs and unprinted works, doctors, artists, French officers on parole, tourists, busybodies. And if he with scant ceremony dismissed sightseers without having dined them he repented his incivility over his first bottle.

Scott had no need to economize. He had sold to Constable the copyrights of all his preceding writings for an immense sum; Constable had tried to stop at ten thousand pounds but Scott had held out for his price and had finally wrested twelve thousand; moreover he had bound Constable not to reveal the authorship of *Waverley* during the author's lifetime under penalty of two thousand pounds. He had reason to congratulate himself on his business acumen. Not so long ago when John Ballantyne's affair had looked black he had come near to sacrificing these copyrights for almost any sum that would avert bankruptcy; he would not have thought then of asking more than four thousand. With high spirits he returned to the Duke of Buccleuch his Grace's guarantee and pointed out his own clever bargain.

He might well say that up to this time his life had been "in all its private and public relations, as fortunate perhaps as was ever lived." He was a lion in Edinburgh, a lion in London. He had been received in London as a celebrity; the Prince Regent had given him a dinner, had toasted him as the author of *Waverley,* had, at his refusal of the toast, respected his anonymity and had toasted him in even more flattering terms. Everything he wrote turned to gold in his hands. His son was entering the cavalry as he would himself have done had he not been lame. His other children were a credit to him; his lands spread about him showing the promise of true magnificence. The baronetcy that had been bestowed upon him just before he was fifty had come as a free gift; he had neither asked for it nor paid for it as other men had. It had come purely as a recognition from the Prince Regent. He was, after all, no obscure private citizen; at Abbotsford he was sheriff, laird, kinglet eminent in his domain. He schemed to erect cottages for a group of honest laborers who would agree to keep houses, gardens, and children neat and clean. He liked the idea of a sort of feudal castle and estate. It pleased him to revive old Scotch customs, to have the hundred children of his

tenantry come to the mansion the day before New Year's
to dance to the pipes for their laird and receive bannocks
and pennies from his bounty, though he never got over
his wonder that his laborers could keep children fed and
clothed on their eighteen or twenty pence a day wages.

His schemes for Abbotsford were more and more
grandiose. He liked the idea of an irregular dwelling
such as had grown up in his additions to the original
farmhouse. Now an architect was devising the new
dwelling with space for all the guests Scott should ever
desire, balconies, ironwork railings with gas lamps over
each post, the newfangled expensive gaslighting for the
whole house, a really large dining room, any number of
bedrooms with dressingrooms (and couches therein for
extra guests), a bowling green, a fountain fed by a spring.
There were, of course, an ample library, a small study,
and a museum for the armor and antiquarian collections.
Stained glass was gathered, orders were sent to London
for glass, for wainscotting, and for various pieces of furniture. There was no attempt at economy.

He was entitled to a castle. He amused himself in devising it in what he called Bravura style. There was a
rich tower; there were notched gables; there were di-
agonal chimneys. Painted glass with the heads of Scottish kings was ordered for the windows of his armory.
He summoned artists to make drawings for his dining
room wainscot. In addition to his other guest rooms he
devised a garret with especially romantic quarters for
artists, poets, actors and such gipsy folk. His books were

bound in blue morocco stamped with his own device and motto, a portcullis and an anagram of his name, *clausus tutus ero.*

In house and without he was surrounded with a pack of dogs. He had given up riding spirited horses, taking rather to a sober cob as he grew older and heavier; but his son Walter, a six-foot giant, took up his father's sports of riding and hunting; and the stable was no mean one. There was no reason for slackening expenses. He could with a light heart add another estate to his holdings, paying cheerfully ten thousand pounds; an estate which added to his already large grounds made him in truth a great laird. He feared somewhat that public opinion would write him down mercenary; but these novels were a mercenary project. Only they happened to be also great fun. It was as much fun to write them as to listen to people's comments and guesses as to their authorship. He himself turned their suspicions to his various friends and to his own brother Thomas still overseas in Canada till he could persuade him to return home to Scotland.

Not only did he deny the authorship but he went further; he reviewed for the *Quarterly* the *Tales of My Landlord,* gravely treating them as the work of an unknown stranger. One of his triumphs these days was the pleading of Jeffrey that he write again for the *Edinburgh Review* and his ability to refuse for the present since he was unable to find time to fill the requests of the *Quarterly* and of the new magazine set up in thriving circumstances by Blackwood. But he agreed to do something for Jeffrey later on.

Not only was he prosperous himself but both Ballantynes were flourishing. Now that all those dead books had been unloaded on Constable, and John was receiving profits from his slight labors as Scott's go-between, the world was apparently smiling on him, too. He led the gayest of lives. He so contrived his fashionable residence that his substantially built wife could not get through the narrow halls leading to his banquet room. Dinners that he served were as elegant as the company he gathered about him. He did not scruple to send to France for truffles and pastries; and the rarest of viands were his favorite diet. He kept fine horses and expensive mistresses. He usually rode up to an auction he was to conduct on a milk white charger named Old Mortality. The other horses of his stable were also named from Scott's characters. He rarely stepped forth even to business without a leash of fine greyhounds. As for himself he went about clad in elegant sporting clothes, light grey coats with silver buttons engraved with horses, foxes, dogs; white breeches; and the most brilliantly polished riding boots. He was an ornament to any auction block. In general a buffoon, he was soberly in earnest as an auctioneer. He carried on his business with the gravity of a parson; and yet was so plausible in his appeals to his audience that he disposed of his goods to better advantage than many a witty fellow. Scott was usually among the crowd, bidding spiritedly for Venetian lamps, Milanese cuirasses, old cabinets, and fine filigree. John Ballantyne kept his fooling for private life. When the drink was in him he would perform drolly, always egged on

by his patron. It amused Scott to see the little fellow
mimic every one from dukes to cobblers; it stirred up his
mirth to see him caper and hear him sing. Rarely did
he take him seriously; John was his clown, his dwarf.
Even his vices were to be laughed at.

John's brother James was also changed by Edinburgh
life and association with the great Sheriff, though his
tastes remained comparatively simple. He had married
a woman of substance — though his doing so did not
discharge his three thousand pound indebtedness to Scott
— and lived in substantial style. His house was not
adorned with fripperies like John's nor did his table
groan with foreign delicacies. He leaned toward solid
things, both furniture and food. When he entertained
his dinners were Scotch in quality and in quantity. On
the eve of the publication of each of Scott's novels he
would give a large dinner the guests at which pretended
to be ignorant of the Great Unknown.

Scott was, of course, the guest of honor at all these dinners; both Scott and Ballantyne nevertheless believed that
no one knew except such friends as Scott himself told.
The feast was always of extraordinary proportions. Tur-
tle and venison were added to an ample menu, and to the
ale of ordinary meals was added iced punch, and old
Madeira. When all had eaten their way through manifold dishes the cloth was drawn; then Ballantyne would
rise solemnly for the first toast:

Fill full !
I drink to the general joy of the whole table !

Hardly had this been swallowed when the second toast came:

> The King, God bless him !

Once more the bottles circulated. James Ballantyne swelled his chest and with beaming countenance and sonorous voice proceeded pompously: "Gentlemen, there is another toast which never has been nor shall be omitted in this house of mine — I give you the health of Mr. Walter Scott with three times three !"

After the enthusiasm of the table had subsided Scott would rise to thank the company and express his affection for the host. Mrs. Ballantyne having sat with them thus far now retired, leaving the gentlemen to stricter attention to the plentiful bottles. After a round of drinks and a burst of general conversation James Ballantyne would rise once more, his hand raised for silence. Clearing his throat he would settle into a fixed attitude, his eyes raised above the company toward some apparently distant spot, the very veins on his forehead swollen with effort. But gone were the stentorian tones of his other toasts; all that issued from his pursed lips was a violent whisper:

> Gentlemen, a bumper to the immortal Author of *Waverley* !

The gentlemen raised their glasses cheering lustily, Scott's glass raised with the rest, his voice, though faint, sharing in the applause.

In the silence as the glasses were drained Ballantyne's voice would rise again. He would lament the obscurity in which the illustrious but too modest author chose to conceal himself from the plaudits of the world; he would thank the company for the manner in which the toast had been received though he had been able to give but the shadow of a name; he would assure them that the author would, when informed of this, be highly gratified. He would divulge the name of the forthcoming novel and ask them to drink to its success. Then, feeling proud of his success at having told so much and no more, Ballantyne would, as he thought, divert the minds of his guests. To this end he would start trolling a song in a highly theatrical manner. Other toasts followed; other drinkers felt impelled to burst into song. Finally Scott would take his departure along with his close friends. Those who remained were special cronies of Ballantyne, who would call for the removal of the claret and the olives and the substitution of grilled bones and a steaming bowl of punch. The departure of the more staid and more honored guests no less than the new libations loosened tongues all round. James would now begin to elaborate on the beauties of the new romance about to burst upon the public.

"Read a chapter on't," his cronies would plead.

"Nay, by'r Lady, nay !" he would cry. But his pleadings were as weak as his voice was fast becoming as the cups filled and refilled. Soon he would go to his desk for the proof-sheets, and would turn them over fondly chuckling to himself. He would read a bit of dialogue to let his friends share the laugh, then another little bit. At last with a mighty hem he would clear his throat and with befogged voice embark upon a reading.

**LADY SCOTT**

*From a painting by James Saxon*

Quite in contrast to these two quondam tradesmen Constable lived in quiet elegance in the suburbs. He drove to and from town in a low-hung green barouche drawn by a pair of well-matched black horses and guided by an elderly coachman in simple blue livery. He had been brought up in wealth; he had no need to flaunt it. The Ballantynes perhaps had need to announce their prosperity to a doubting world. James, to be sure, was content with a fashionable carriage drawn by one powerful cob; but John, when he was not capering about on a mettlesome hunter, rode in a bright blue dog-cart drawn by two prancing horses; and more often than not as he rattled to the races there sat beside him some notoriously successful and expensive actress.

Constable might at times seem vain, at times despotic — Scott had long since dubbed him Czar — but Constable was a gentleman. He lived with the quiet ease of custom.

For Walter Scott the antics of the Ballantynes were an outlet. His boisterous spirits were curbed often enough with the grand company among whom his lot was now cast; the days of his own fooling were far behind him. The Ballantynes acted the clown for him; he could laugh at and with them without endangering his dignity. Besides, the one thing he must avoid, now that he was a baronet, was the sin of priggishness; he must not become a snob and forget old friends.

He did not overvalue baubles, but he was rich, he was great, he had made his faithful Charlotte Lady Scott. "Your honours," he wrote her from London, "will be gazetted on Saturday."

# CHAPTER V

A T fifty Scott had, as he was fond of saying, "more of fame and fortune than mere literature ever procured for a man before." He wrote his son Walter: "I have been more successful in life than most people, and know well how much success depends, first upon desert, and then on knowledge of the *carte de pays.*"

The handsome six-foot lad was none too fond of his father's admonitions; he was off on his chosen career of military man, a career his father granted him because he remembered his own youthful longings, though he would now have preferred to see his sons follow his own footsteps in law and literature. Neither, however, was so inclined. Charles was a merry, idle lad, unwilling while under his father's roof to apply himself to classic learning; he had to be sent to the house of a worthy clergyman to be prepared for university. Scott had been reluctant to break up the family circle he loved, but it was already broken by the departure of Walter, a sportsman whose company and gun he missed. Many were the letters he sent, begging for news, urgent of good morals and economy. Perhaps Walter would have gladly dispensed with some of the magnificence of his inheritance in order to escape the constant warnings against extravagance. Each fifty pounds went to him with a tag of prudential

would retire to write a few swift chapters to dispatch
to James Ballantyne's presses before he returned to play
host to the company gathered at Abbotsford.

Everything in life, except repose, was delightful to him.
His thinking he did on foot or on horseback. His writing was an athletic exercise, so swiftly did he push pen
over paper, so quick was he to start up to search out a reference, so thoroughly did he enter into the activities of
his imaginary characters. He did not understand repose. When he talked he indulged in pantomime. If
he could not be tramping or galloping he was not therefore still. As he listened to guests or talked business or
delighted his visitor with tales, fantastic or merry, he
would stack up books or arrange letters, or twist papers
into matches as he sat at his desk. He would snap his
fingers, beckon to a dog, play with its ears, pat its head;
then jumping up he would open the door to let the dogs
out, whereupon his huge old cat would solemnly climb
down from a stepladder and curl up on his knees to be
stroked.

Life had truly dealt richly by him. He had been received by all the great in London; princes had visited
him at Abbotsford, princes and poets, and friends. He
had been the guest of Wellington abroad and at home;
he had received from that great general praises which he
valued almost more than those of anyone else. He had
dined with royalty; he had been given a baronetcy not
along with a dozen others, merchants and generals, but
by himself, the title a free gift in recognition of his accomplishments. He had been offered honorary degrees

by both Cambridge and Oxford; he was president of the Royal Society of Edinburgh.

He pursued his pet scheme of the building at Abbotsford with every confidence in the continuance of his superb luck. There had been clouds on his horizon now and then; illness had threatened to check his career at its height. He had disregarded the first warnings; but one night at dinner with many guests he had had a warning he could not disregard. So great had the pain become that to his own horror and that of his guests he had rushed from the room roaring. Nothing his frightened wife and the almost equally perplexed doctors could do brought relief for many a long hour. It was some time before strength returned. Meanwhile the doctors had blistered and bled to their hearts' content until the stout giant who took to his bed rose a thin ghost of himself, his hair whitened and his frame hung with flabby flesh. But though he had attacks again and again he finally kept them under control when a new doctor discovered that all his woes could be remedied with calomel.

Yet he had not been daunted even by pain. As soon as he obtained any relief at all he turned his attention to his novels. If he could not hold a pen, why then he must have an amanuensis. *Rob Roy* went ahead by dictation, though its creator sometimes protested to James Ballantype when he came begging for completed sheets, that the curmurrings of his guts would cause Rob's early demise.

*Rob Roy* was named by Constable who from now on had his own ideas of titles, and usually managed to wrest his choice from Scott. The fat little publisher was very vain of his connection with Scott, and quite believed in Scott's ability to keep on writing indefinitely in a vein that would be perennially popular. Even when the novels ceased to sell at the same enormous rate the moment they appeared Constable never lost his faith in them; and he forebore to stress to their author their lesser popularity. He was indefatigable in suggesting topics for new novels and in furnishing bibliographies of historical material. He would strut up and down his office with smug satisfaction whenever his suggestions were accepted, boasting to Cadell, his partner: "By God, I am all but the author of the Waverley Novels !"

John Ballantyne, snugly comfortable on his unearned profits from the novels, shared Constable's feeling of proprietorship. He saw the years before him increasing in prosperity through the popularity of his friend and patron. He watched the extension of grounds and the erection of the castle at Abbotsford with interest; he, too, would become a builder. He had always retained a fondness for his native town of Kelso; there he would go and erect a lordly summer home of his own.

Not far from ducal parks he found at the end of the long village street three quaint old houses with notched gables and thatched roofs. In one of these he made a comfortable set of bachelor quarters where he might take pleasant refuge while his extensive building operations went on. The other houses he converted into grand stables for his many horses and dogs. Having made himself and his livestock comfortable he proceeded with his

JOHN GIBSON LOCKHART
*After a painting by Sir Francis Grant*

ARCHIBALD CONSTABLE
*From a painting by Sir Henry Raeburn*

mansion, which was to stand back from the street in well-laid out grounds. The entrance was lordly; it led into a hall sacred to his favorite sport of angling; there was to be a bust of Piscator and the walls were to be decorated with various piscatorial emblems. The spacious drawing and dining rooms were to overlook an Italian garden with ornamental steps down the many terraces to the river. Perhaps a bower there where guests might enjoy the magnificent views. Already the fountain had been erected, copied after Scott's own, with a pretty height of falling water.

Here John dined Scott and Lockhart, vividly describing the beauties and grandeurs yet to come. With brimming bumpers they drank the success of his Walton Hall. Scott's heart as usual warmed to the merry little man. John needed protection; if he were to indulge in all this building he would obviously need a bigger income. Scott's fertile brain had a scheme instantly at hand. Long ago he had thought of a Novelist's Library, reprints of Defoe, Richardson, Smollet, Sterne, and the like. Here was a project that could go on for years, that required little effort, and that was bound to be a money-maker. John's enthusiasm was immediate. He always had a ready appreciation of projects that required the minimum of work and the maximum of profit. Scott would, of course, write the prefaces. That would insure their success. All John had to do was to assemble the texts and see them through the press.

Three days later when John paid a friendly visit to Sir Walter he was astonished to have put in his hands the

completed preface to Fielding's novels, a deftly written
life of the author.  Others followed faster than the jester
could take care of them and Ballantyne's Novelist's Library was launched upon a world which had become
somewhat prudish.  It showed a marked preference for
the purity of Scott's own novels as against the broadness
of the older writers.  Constable was willing to father
this as all other schemes of Sir Walter's but the project
was before long allowed to die.

There was, indeed, no longer reason for its existence,
when merry, careless John Ballantyne had passed from
this world of gaiety and mischief.  He lay on his death-
bed with the proof-sheets of a volume of the Novelist's
Library spread out on the coverlet, mute testimony of
his industry; upon them lay his last will and testament,
signed just before Sir Walter hurried into the room.
Struggling with a cough he held out a wasted hand to the
hearty giant.  This was the end.  He would not live to
enjoy his country home; Sir Walter would, however, live
many a long year to enjoy Abbotsford.  He would have
liked to complete both his home and this Library; he
did like to finish tasks he had begun.  It was not to be.
Overcome with self-pity and coughing he lay back, to
rise and read his will.  Two thousand pounds he was
bequeathing to Sir Walter, enough to add materially, he
felt, to the magnificence of the library at Abbotsford.
He began a detailed description of the elaborate book-
shelves he desired; and outlined the best arrangement for
them in the big room.  He became as eloquent as ever
he had been on the platform auctioning off the finest of

French baubles. But his breath failed him; soon he was too weak to talk. Standing at the side of the newmade grave Sir Walter said softly, "I feel as if there would be less sunshine for me from this day forth."

He was, however, never one to dwell on grief; the immediate present claimed him too fully for retrospection. The present was good; he did not lose its savor by dwelling on the sadness that was past. He was fortunate to have known John and to have enjoyed so much of his company. John had been the jolliest of companions; quick of mind and tongue, quick of body; a gay, thoughtless chap, giving on the whole pleasure more often than pain. Improvident, yes; his faults were many; but then so were his virtues. Never was a more admiring and devoted friend. And he would long chuckle over John's merry prescription to the pale student:

"Art sick, lad?"

"Ay, verra sick, sir."

"Ah weel, try this draught, my lad. 'Tis unco guid taken on an empty stomach!" and he had pressed a five-pound note into the boy's hand.

That his own hand was worse than empty when he died was only to be expected with a man of such easy temper. The two thousand pounds grandiloquently bequeathed to the Abbotsford library were purely imaginary. John died as he had lived, heavily in debt. His intentions had been good, he had meant to benefit his benefactor.

It was pleasanter and kinder to remember these things than the old annoyances of the publishing business. On the whole he had come out of that very well; not every one would have been clever enough to get rid of all the unsold stock.   Constable had been lucky enough to get him on any terms.   He had indeed, exhausted his vein of poetry — after all he could never have stripped himself for the public as Byron did; he would rather not command the wonder of the public by exhibiting himself as the dying gladiator.   Let Byron hold the field; he had no reticence; his genius was the more powerful.   For himself he was "no great believer in poetical immortality."   He had had his day as a poet; and he had been sensible enough to be satisfied; he had not continued in a vein when it showed signs of exhaustion.   Probably Byron was the better poet.   But he had reaped a fine harvest; and he had not been bankrupt of resources.   The public appetite for these novels which he wrote so rapidly was apparently insatiable.

If he needed anything to bolster his belief in his moneymaking powers, there was Constable's enthusiasm. Constable, too, was engaging in extensive building operations, and was, besides, beguiling his weeks in London buying curiosities for Abbotsford: portraits of Scottish kings, elaborately carved boxwood chairs from the Borghese Palace at Rome, slabs of mosaic suitable for hearthstones.   These things he offered as incidental gifts: "Our literary connection is too important to make it necessary for your publishers to trouble you about the pounds, shillings, and pence of such things"; they were gifts.   And Constable prowled about London in search of more antiques to add to the Abbotsford collections.

He had only to hear a whisper of a new novel projected to offer a thousand pounds' advance upon it.

Meantime it would, Constable thought, be a good idea while *Peveril of the Peak* went through the press for Ballantyne to run off new editions of Scott's various publications, for instance, ten volumes miniature of his poetical works, twelve volumes of novels and tales, six volumes of historical romances, and say a stray volume of poems taken from the novels. Five thousand copies of these requiring nearly eight thousand reams of paper for the total of 145,000 volumes enough, in faith, to keep the good Ballantyne printing at top speed for many a long day, especially as he would need to turn out thirty or forty thousand of each new novel that fell from Scott's pen. Prosperity for them all; that was the one sure thing in life.

"My house," sang Sir Walter, "is enlarged beyond what is necessary, but Constable's voice says, like the cackle of the hens to the old woman, as translated by the children in Scotland — 'Buy tobacco — buy tobacco — I'll pay a.' " Golden eggs were these of Scott's laying; so much did Constable believe in them that he advanced more and more money for Scott to pour out upon Abbotsford, his romantic dream of a manor house. And when Constable had a momentary tremor at the thought of having paid over ten thousand pounds for novels neither begun nor named, *Quentin Durward* leapt forward with a sale that proved Scott's popularity in its zenith. Germany had joined Britain's choruses of praise long since; now Paris took up the cry.

Success was there in the form in which it could not be doubted, good round coins of gold. When Scott urged his son again and again to manage his affairs with prudence, to be neither stingy nor extravagant, he was, he thought, showing him an example. He did, indeed, spend freely in order to build up this estate for his son's inheritance; but he was in no way exceeding his prospective income. As long as the public read he could add turret to tower, wall to garden; he could ornament an oratory, fit in a secret staircase, follow what architectural whim he would.

He was saddened again and again by the death of old friends but it was no part of his philosophy to spend time in grief. It was better to turn one's thought toward the enjoyment of those who remained.

His good friend and neighbor was enlivening the late days of his life with a bride; Scott allowed him a quiet Sabbath but on the Monday morning he sent over all his menservants with a motley array of pipes and noisemakers to serenade the new married pair, he himself hovering near on his pony to see the fun. For he never lost his taste for boyish fooling.

And soon he had a chance to indulge his fondness for a grand show. The King decided to pay Scotland a visit. Scarcely had the news spread than the royal yacht was seen in the harbor. Off in the rain Scott hastened to offer greetings. He was received on board with a hearty welcome; his Majesty pledged his health in a bumper of the Scotch national drink, draining a glass of neat whiskey. Having emptied his own glass to his

KING GEORGE IV ENTERING HOLYROOD

*From a painting by Sir David Wilkie*

Majesty's health, Scott was emboldened to ask for the glass emptied by royal lips, as an heirloom for his children. Carefully disposing it in his cloak he went back to complete the arrangements for the royal welcome.

At home he found one of his random guests, this time the shy clergyman-poet Crabbe with whom he began to converse with his usual eloquence. Indeed if Scott wrote poems and novels with unusual rapidity the reason lay in the fact that he talked his incidents and descriptions; having talked them out he had only to transcribe them and the composition was done.

Crabbe was somewhat intimidated by the very warmth of his welcome. He sat perched nervously on the edge of his chair while his host strove to draw him into the conversation. The very heartiness of Scott made Crabbe feel more insignificant and silent. His host threw back his coat to settle back at ease in his great chair. Suddenly he sprang up with a scream that brought Lady Scott instantly to his side.

"Is it the stomach, Scott?" she cried anxiously.

"Nay, nay," her good man moaned, " 'tis another place. I e'en forgot his Majesty's cup and sat on't." And he ruefully emptied from his pockets the splinters of glass; and retired to have his wound dressed by the solicitous Lady Scott.

This was the only untoward circumstance of the royal visit. Scott was in charge of the arrangements of welcome which he directed on the same large scale as the Waverley novels. Here was his chance to arrange real men on the streets of Edinburgh, write his pageantry with lery" boarded above to permit hanging old guns, old portraits, old armor, and odds and ends of antiquity. For the drawingroom and library came finely pencilled cedar wood, beautifully colored like gingerbread. The splendid Chinese paper in sheets twelve feet high proved to be enough for two bedrooms beside the drawingroom.

The gift that attracted the most attention was a chair made of all the good wood left in the crumbling house where the great Wallace, betrayed, had met death. This chair was so loudly heralded that the gift assumed almost national significance. The first stage of its journey, down to the river to be borne to Abbotsford, was a triumphal progress; the town band playing *Scots Wha Hae wi' Wallace Bled* preceded it; and there followed a cheering, singing crowd. Both before and after its safe journey the Wallace chair was the centre of pilgrimages.

But Sir Walter did not rely on gifts for his magnificence within this castle of his, this "place to dream of, not to tell." He ordered through the agency of his kind actor-friend Terry tables of the finest marble, mirrors of elegance, silk damask for curtains to be finished off with quantities of gold fringe. For the library he had curtains of crimson made from finely woven wool of his own sheep. He summoned upholsterers to make the curtains and to cover chairs and sofas, under his own direction. He summoned artists to paint his ceilings, carved antique oak relieved by coats of arms at the intersections of the beams. The cornices were plaster of paris painted to look like the most antique of polished woods. For these coats of arms he drew upon all the families with which his an-

SIR WALTER SCOTT AND A GROUP OF HIS FRIENDS

*From a painting at Abbotsford*

cestry was connected and the families of his closest friends. The college of heraldry was consulted that they might all be strictly accurate.

To light up his mansion Sir Walter installed one of the newfangled gas-lighting systems which were one of his minor business ventures. He believed in the virtues of the new lighting sufficiently not only to install it himself but to act as director of a company and investor in it. The gas had to be made on the premises, and stored in a tank connected, of course, with chandeliers each of which kept small pilot lights burning. One of Sir Walter's pleasures after the completion of Abbotsford was to have a large party dining at the close of a day. No one would notice the little red pilot lights while the sun was up. Gradually the twilight would deepen; and then at the turning of a screw the huge room would be flooded with brilliant light. Exclamations of surprise and delight would burst from all. And Sir Walter could expatiate on the virtues of his new toy. He himself loved brilliant light; his sober son-in-law doubted its being either good for the eyes or in correct taste. It was a bit dashing, a bit too exuberant. Besides it smelled vilely. Sir Walter being blunt of taste and smell was as ignorant of its annoying odor as he was of that of the strong venison sometimes served at his table. And he took unaffected joy in the Arabian Nights appearance of his palace bathed in fairy light from cellar to attic. It pleased him that all the world came to stare.

Even his patience and courtesy were, however, tried by the sightseeing parties which sometimes amounted to and recommending that he read the first scene of the *Merry Wives of Windsor,* assuming himself to be Abraham Slender who says: "I will marry her, sir, at your request: but if there be no great love in the beginning, yet heaven may decrease it upon better acquaintance, when we are married and have more occasion to know one another." It is plain that Sir Walter had forgotten his own methods of wooing, his own methods of falling into love with a whole heart. His son was not, of course, to be coerced; Sir Adam Ferguson might be told:

> His thoughts were still on honor bent;
> He never stooped to love;
> No lady in the land has power
> His frozen heart to move.

Nevertheless he had better take the summer off at Abbotsford.

Young Walter was amenable. He came, he saw, he dug up an attachment on the basis of previous summers, he wooed and won. He agreed with his father's Shakespearean postscript: "Five hundred pounds and possibilities are good gifts." Jane's tiny person had many more than five hundred pounds to give it weight. And she was quite willing to marry the six-foot bearded hussar. Sir Walter with satisfaction counted one more daughter in his brood. His house was founding; Walter would marry this mite of attractive femininity and her fortune and estate added to his inheritance of Abbotsford would make a noble property for *his* heir. He foresaw a line of Walter Scotts, baronets, rich and mighty men.

His happiness reflected itself in the New Year's party of 1825 to which everybody was welcome. The whole countryside apparently availed itself of the privilege to drink the New Year in with health and prosperity to Abbotsford and its builder. Next week Sir Walter gave a ball to announce his son's engagement; a ball that permitted the illumination of the castle and an entertainment on a truly lavish scale. All these merriments added to the time taken to settle the interior of the house had sadly cut into his writing time; he had been too busy to sit even the accustomed hours at his desk; but he would make up for his idle pen by renewed attention; he would write the faster for this interruption. He would need to make up these enormous outlays; and then Jane's pretty estate could be made prettier. The approach to the house could be made more picturesque; with Jane's consent he would like to build a new road there; he would, gladly, undertake all the labor of supervision and all the expense while she stayed in Ireland with her young husband.

While he dreamt of the grandson who should perpetuate his name he played great games with little Johnie Lockhart, the frail child who listened eagerly to Sir Walter's tales. Grandpa bought him the tiniest of ponies, permitting him to ride about in the huge rooms and halls of Abbotsford; trotting under the library table, a huge affair constructed under Sir Walter's own eye in the very room in which it stood.

These were happy days. He sat with Lady Scott by the fireside, a strong man of fifty-four enjoying the magnificence of the present, sentimentally attached to the simplicity of the past. They had been happy at Lasswade, too, where he had built tables and bowers with his own hands. But she had known he would succeed; she knew when she married him that he would be a great rich man. He had not disappointed her in anything; he had been the most cheerful of companions, the tenderest of husbands, the most successful of men. They had founded a valiant line. It gave them both pleasure to sign over Abbotsford to their son in his marriage settlements. Abbotsford was now an hereditary estate; theirs was a life interest in it; it would, as was proper, devolve upon their son; and in time upon his son and upon generation after generation of Sir Walter Scotts. Life had dealt with them kindly, generously. They had years before them now in which to enjoy the fulness of their achievement.

The immediate pleasure at hand in 1825 was a trip to Ireland to visit Captain Walter and his bride. Lady Scott was too timid a traveller, too dependent upon home comforts to risk the journey; Sophia felt that her duty lay with taking her weak little son to the seashore; Charles, the Oxford student, elected for himself a journey to the Highlands; and so Abbotsford was to rest in idleness for two months. Sir Walter set off to enjoy the deep satisfaction of being the guest of his son's table, taking with him in his comfortable carriage his daughter Anne and his son-in-law Lockhart upon whose shoulders rested the responsibilities of baggage and servants, lodgings and money — no small matter this last since when Sir Walter

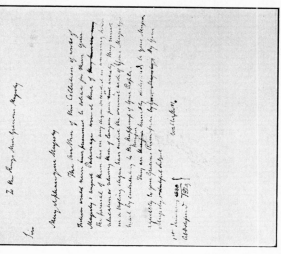

DRAFT OF A LETTER IN THE HANDWRITING
OF SIR WALTER SCOTT

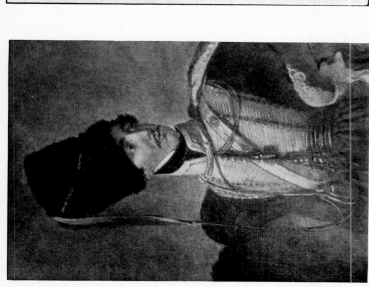

SIR WALTER SCOTT
THE NOVELIST'S SON

*From a painting by Sir William Allan*

had made his son a present of one hundred pounds he rounded out the trip's expenses to a good five hundred pounds. Anne had the embarrassment of being addressed now as Mrs. Lockhart, now as Lady Scott, which her menfolk thought rather hard on her, since it prevented the coming forward of suitors.

The Irish journey was an ovation from the start. From the Lord-Lieutenant, the Marquis Wellesley, down to the street beggars, everyone was eager to pay homage to the Great Unknown; even now Sir Walter kept up the fiction of not being the author of the Waverley Novels; so that when an Irish librarian referred to "your *Redgauntlet*" he answered, "Sir, I have not happened to meet such a book."

His denials did not injure his popularity; if he preferred being fêted as a poet, the Irish were willing to fall in with his humor. The University gave him an LL.D.; the notables outdid themselves in entertainments for his honor. He had only to appear in a street to have pedestrians line up on the curb, shopkeepers and their wives bowing and curtseying at their shop doors. If he went into a shop leaving his carriage at the curb, he came out to find himself surrounded with cheering crowds; his carriage moved off hampered by his admirers, and his progress was like that of royalty. Shaking his head a sober Bailie looked after him: "Yon was owre like worshipping the creature," he said sadly.

Worship it was beyond doubt. When Sir Walter went to the theatre the house upon perceiving him was instantly in an uproar. The curtain rose in a perfect hubbub; the actors mights as well have had no tongues. Twice the leading actress left the stage; twice she came back vainly trying to be heard. Finally the manager himself mounted the stage, and shouted for silence. Having got, if not silence, at least a let up in the roar he called out:

"Good friends, what is the cause of this great noise ?"

A thousand throats shouted: "Sir Walter Scott !"

Up to this time Sir Walter had sat pretending for nearly an hour to be ignorant of his being the object of this tribute. Now he rose.

"I am sure the Irish people," here he was interrupted by a tremendous cheer — "I am sure this respectable audience will not suppose that a stranger can be insensible to the kindness of their reception of him, and if I have been too long in saying this, I trust it will be attributed to the right cause — my unwillingness to take upon me honors so distinguished, and which I could not and cannot but feel to be unmerited."

Such modesty was greeted with even greater cheering. In vain did the manager urge his distinguished guest to occupy the stage box. Sir Walter sat quietly until throats wearied and the play was allowed to proceed.

He had come to Ireland chiefly to enjoy seeing his son a householder, a Captain. He was amused at Walter's way of life, the atmosphere of a barrack town being little different from that of Oxford. Walter and his fellow officers though with little coin in their purses led a merry ample life, well fed, well housed, well mounted. Their fraternal relations led them to share practically everything they owned save their toothbrushes and wives. Walter's father was well pleased. Walter was no longer insensible to his father's fame, though he had no literary leanings himself; he no longer felt as he had in his earlier days when he had thrashed a schoolfellow for calling him the Lady of the Lake. His little wife was all that her father-in-law could desire, a sweet little listener whose merry laugh always rang at the right point in his stories.

There were gay excursions of all of the family party to visit Miss Edgeworth and her father; a week's admiration of the literary lady in her native haunts where the schoolchildren comported themselves on her father's lawn, turned into a public park for all the villagers. They gathered Miss Edgeworth and part of her family in, increasing their cavalcade, to pay homage to as many of the beauties of Ireland as possible. Wherever Sir Walter's name was heard there he received the most flattering of tributes.

Turning toward home he paused at the Lakes to renew acquaintance with Southey and Wordsworth. Wordsworth as a venerable old man made him momentarily feel himself to be aging. In the excitement of the days that made up his visit he hardly noted how Wordsworth patronized him; with his usual kindliness he enjoyed Wordsworth's harping on Wordsworth's poetry; and when the old man paused in his recital of his own verses, Sir Walter would begin reciting them himself. But there was no mistaking the tribute to Scott when some half hundred boats circled round him on a day's excursion to the islands. Again and again he heard himself cheered; whenever his boat approached two little cannon puffed valiantly; and two bands circled about him valiantly playing different tunes. Wordsworth, though he might ignore Scott's claim as brother poet, though he might refuse to recognize the claims of Byron, though he might limit poesy to his own writings, nevertheless had to admit Scott's enormous popularity even in the vicinity of Rydal Mount. Personally, of course, he was all that was friendly; and it was Lockhart, not Sir Walter, who was offended at his omission to mention *Marmion*.

At home once more, in the fall of 1825, Scott heard Abbotsford ring with good cheer. The Walter Scott who moved jovially among his many guests, who rode about his lands, planning, exhibiting, chatting with tenants and workmen, was less agile than the Walter Scott of a quarter of a century ago. Though the years had dealt with him kindly, he was stiffer of limb, heavier of body; he could no longer vault upon a spirited horse to go galloping about the country; he was no longer young — young, that is, in body; in mind he was as young as ever. Anecdote and tale ran forever in his head, ran trippingly from his tongue or pen. He could still charm any audience whether of high or low degree. He was at home with his ducal guests and with his humble tenants. His life had been a steady progression; twenty-five years ago at Lasswade he had been entertaining penniless young lawyers like himself. Now his almost regal palace housed marchionesses and dukes.

The house was well filled when up to the gates drew three grand carriages disgorging a whole bevy of servants to attend their mistress the enormously wealthy Mrs. Coutts (the quondam actress in a provincial troupe before her marriage to England's great banker), now a widow wooed by the Duke of St. Albans who with his sister completed her immediate party — out of consideration to the perplexed Lady Scott she had left in Edinburgh four of the seven carriages with which she was making her Scotch tour. Somehow they were all tucked into Abbotsford, the two physicians (two lest one should himself fall ill on the trip), the meek lady companion, the two lady's maids (one to work and one to watch by night, lest ghosts come); somehow Scott prevailed upon the good nature of his titled guests to be kind to the good lady who departed after three days enormously pleased with herself and her host.

And now the castle became strangely silent. When Sir Walter came out for Christmas he was alone with his wife and his daughter Anne. The Lockharts had taken themselves to London where Lockhart had accepted the editorship of the *Quarterly Review* at the instance of Murray the bookseller and the youthful Benjamin Disraeli whose talents made him at nineteen Murray's confidant and adviser. Sir Walter rejoiced at the financial plum, he hoped the warmer winters would offset the loss of country air for his pet, the delicate Johnie, but he missed the trio. He would miss his son-in-law, too, in the tiresome researches for the *Life of Napoleon*. This historical stuff took the time of a dozen novels. He was wearing his eyes out over fine print and difficult manuscripts. He had to take notes on all this reading; it was immensely more difficult than to spin off a romance, writing with one hand and stroking a favorite dog with the other. To relieve the strain he divided his time, weaving the story of *Woodstock* on the side.

For though his estate was large enough, his house finished, his eldest son a captain, his nephew well placed on the road to success, he could not rest. There was a large bordering estate likely to come on the market for forty or fifty thousand pounds; why not add that to Abbotsford and make the holding still more lordly? He had never felt better in his life; to be sure he could no longer tramp or ride at the old rate or for the same length of time, but he could still fell a tree and swing an ax with the strength of a young man. His mind was still fertile. His wife's illnesses now and then caused a fear to rise in his heart; but they always terminated happily; and the smooth current of undisturbed content flowed on.

That Christmas, after dinner, with the mince pies hardly swallowed, he had a return of his old complaint, being stricken with a sharp illness. "None of my misfortunes," he wrote with good humor, and with such truth as he could not suspect, "happen like those of any one else, for I always break down at the top of my gallop, and when I least expect it."

Nothing was farther from his thoughts than disaster.

# CHAPTER VI

*My life has been in all its private and public relations, as fortunate perhaps as was ever lived, up to this period; and whether pain or misfortune may lie behind the dark curtain of futurity, I am already a sufficient debtor to the bounty of Providence to be resigned to it.*

— WALTER SCOTT.

## CHAPTER VI

SICKNESS brought a pause; perhaps it would be "Goodnight Sir Walter about sixty." After all, he mused, he had lived. He was now fifty-four; he had had more success than most men, certainly more than any other man of letters; his success had been not only in fame, but in substantial gold. Other men had built up reputations though none had received public acclaim in such generous volume as he; and none had, like him, built up a mighty estate, a mighty fortune.

Recently uncomfortable rumors of financial distress in London had reached Edinburgh. Hurst and Robinson, the London booksellers who acted as Constable's English agents, had imprudently speculated in hops; they were said to have invested one hundred thousand pounds much of which would be a complete loss. If this were true there might be trouble for Constable; and if their losses came back on Constable, his loss would come back to some extent upon James Ballantyne, which meant Sir Walter Scott, the monied man of the printing company. There was small room for doubt but that if Hurst and Robinson actually failed, Constable would be dragged down in their ruin. This would seriously distress the affairs of the Canongate Press which were inextricably interwoven with those of Constable. Still a man of Sir Walter's vast means need not be unduly perturbed over such rumors; if worst came to worst he would, thank God, have enough to pay forty shillings in the pound for any obligations to which Constable's necessities would make him liable.

He did not like his connection with the business world when things failed to run smoothly. He ought, he reflected sadly, to have taken warning over that financial crisis of eleven years ago. He had been cross enough then with James and John Ballantyne over their mismanagement of both businesses; he had thought to lose large sums in settling up the publishing concern, John Ballantyne and Company. Only by the craftiest of dealing had he come off in that affair; curiously enough he might never have finished *Waverley* had it not been for stern necessity. Through that and its successors he had not only made enormous sums of money, but had bargained off the losses of the publishing house. So had good come out of seeming evil.

He had been plagued enough at the time ! He had wanted to clear out of the printing business, too. Perhaps it was to be regretted that he had not stuck to his original determination and withdrawn from the company; he had been stern enough with poor James; he had ordered him to find a monied partner and release him. But he had not been able to withstand James; he had not broken off his connection. He had permitted James to transfer the entire business to him, James acting merely as salaried manager for some years. And then he had readmitted James to partnership. The success of the Waverley Novels had brought such enormous prosperity that he had ceased to be cautious in any way. When money came in fast there seemed no need of close scrutiny of the firm's affair.

Actually at this moment he did not know how things stood; for years Constable had been in the habit of signing the firm's bills; each time he did so, Ballantyne signed a bill of equal amount which Constable was to hold, and to use only if Ballantyne failed to meet the bill signed for him. Sir Walter had not followed these transactions on paper; he did not know now how much of Ballantyne's paper Constable held at this moment. It might be that Constable held bills which were not rightly due because the firm had already met the obligations they guaranteed. It was all very puzzling, like that affair James had had with the wine-merchant. James had paid double in that affair; both the bill to the merchant and the bill to his guarantor; a stupid arrangement. One could hope, however, that there was no such tangle in the matter of bills signed by Ballantyne and Company; it wouldn't be pleasant to be liable for twice their obligations.

He wished he knew the actual state of the firm's finances. Perhaps it would have been wiser if he had spent his time at the office looking over the books; he had always meant to. But he had always drifted off on to his literary schemes, and the details of his writing; he had always liked to try out on James his characters and incidents. If he could make James laugh he could be sure of his humor. James had been a valuable critic. He had always meant to talk business. Somehow he never had.

Yet he was a good business man. He had many a time brought Constable, and Murray, and Longman, and Blackwood to terms. When John Ballantyne would come to him with their offers for a poem or novel, with their suggestions for changes in plot or character, he had sometimes been tactfully obstinate; sometimes — and more often, he had retorted with proper spirit. James had once transmitted to him a proposal of Blackwood's for an alteration in the ending of the plot of the *Black Dwarf;* the fellow had actually offered to bear the expense of cancelling and reprinting the necessary number of sheets ! as if expense had anything to do with the matter. He could hardly help his plots from being inconsistent in minor points, writing as he did; writing with him meant merely transcribing the tales he had retailed to James, or had amused his own hours of journeying with. He needed only to describe the people he had actually met in his travels, combining, intensifying, amplifying; and weave their romance in with the tales he gathered on those same journeys. Of course he could write rapidly. And he rarely needed to look back; he could with safety send sheafs of manuscript off to James to print while he went on with the next chapter; and then that would be set up while he wrote the next and the next. What right had Blackwood to suggest revision ?

"Dear James," he had written, "I have received Blackwood's impudent proposal. G — d — his soul ! Tell

him and his coadjutor that I belong to the Black Hussars
of Literature, who neither give nor receive criticism. I'll
be cursed but this is the most impudent proposal that
ever was made."

After all he had constantly made publishers come to his
terms; he had been the dictator; even Constable for all
his grandiose airs had been humble enough before him.
Just now Constable was obviously troubled. He had
come out to Abbotsford looking comically like a lame
duck trying to make his way on land. He was troubled,
yes; but he was resolute in his assurances that all would
be well. He had, it seemed, carried on with Hurst and
Robinson a cross transaction of signing bills similar to his
arrangement with Ballantyne.

On the whole Constable thought it wisest to support
Hurst and Robinson as well as they could. He himself
had already sent them five thousand pounds, and he now
asked Scott to go surety with him on a loan of five thousand pounds. He could easily raise that much on the
combined security of Scott and himself, and then with
ten thousand pounds the London firm ought to pull
itself out of any hole. Ballantyne and Cadell who were
present at this interview both advised him to oblige Constable. Sir Walter feared that he might be sending good
money after bad; on the other hand he ought to be
guided by these men who were business men first and
foremost and not like himself, merely incidentally concerned with business. Anyhow it would be neither safe
nor courteous at such a time to break with them. Sign he
did. And in all his later embarrassments the loss of this

five thousand pounds, a mere drop in the bottomless bucket, was the one reproach he had for Constable.

For the time being this expedient, however, promised well. Ballantyne came again to talk business, assuring him that all was bound to go smoothly. Nevertheless Sir Walter decided that it might be well for him to economize; he had a sufficiently great estate; he had no real need of more land. He had his dream of a castle; he really did not need to undertake any more building operations. He had enough books and curiosities as it was; he could stop this constant collecting. He would draw in his horns, and rest, and so disregard these claps of thunder. He could economize in other ways more easily; he could get rid of some of these tiresome guests; it was annoying to have strangers quarter themselves on him all the time, mere toadies, some of them; and whereas some of them proved pleasant guests, many of them came only to stare. They were worse than an expense; they were a downright nuisance. Then he could with better cheer deny the fantastic petitions that flooded his mail. Students at Oxford and Cambridge frequently invited him to contribute twenty, fifty, or a hundred pounds to their purses. Literary ladies in distress asked sometimes for money, sometimes merely the use of his name on their title pages to insure the sale of poem or novel. In the past whereas he had always refused to father their literature, he had usually softened his refusal with a remittance.

A Captain of the Danish naval service desiring to help free the province of Colombia dreamt that Sir Walter made him a gift of the funds. He wrote his dream and his request. Perhaps if it were not for these rumors, which Lockhart wrote were gathering strength in London, he might have indulged the fellow. Now the dream would have to go by contraries.

Indeed Lockhart wrote that Constable, whom Scott believed rooted like the oak, was tottering on the verge of ruin; Constable's London banker, it was said, had refused his account. Sir Walter ordered his carriage at once. Constable himself assured him that the rumor was false; Constable was firm as the mountain; he would lose money through this wretched business of Hurst and Robinson; but he would not founder, no not he. He had his faults but he was an honest man. He was indeed too vain a man to fall into a pit. Any man of such arrogant pride would watch his step; he would never have followed a path leading to ruin. Sir Walter was sure that he could trust this despot; Constable would weather the storm.

Perhaps he ought to look into the affairs of Ballantyne and Company immediately. Pshaw ! there was no reason for pettifogging; James was solid enough; why plague him ? That affair of 1814 had threatened ruin; and it had been followed by such prosperity as none of them had dreamt of, all flowing from his pen. Such profits could not melt in thin air.

The printing presses had been rushed to capacity constantly; they could not have failed to be stoutly prosperous. He had kept them busy enough in all conscience himself; and Constable had kindly used them for his manifold projects. Constable was an energetic soul; and a sanguine one. He was always sure that anything he undertook would conquer the world. Well, many of his schemes had conquered the world; he had a right to be sanguine. His *Edinburgh Review* from the start had been an unparalleled success; and then he had made of Scott's poetry and novels a financial nine days' wonder. Perhaps he had published overly much; he had attempted editions and authors who had brought scant returns or none.

Nevertheless all authors owed him thanks; for he had put literature on a paying basis. These young poets, essayists, what not, were reaping the fruits of his efforts; they were being paid far beyond anything writers could have dreamt of when Constable first took the field. His generosity had established many a writer; it had as was right come back to him multiplied. And here he had a dazzling new scheme, a cheap Miscellany which would put the best of the literature of both past and present before the public in editions priced for the moderate purse. Constable said rightly that people ought to be educated in the idea that books were a necessary part of their house furnishings. Now they spent their money on cheap ornaments, cheap pictures; if they could get books cheaply they might be induced to buy them; and books were lasting possessions unlike their present trumpery. He would certainly put cheap books on the market; he would further the education of his country at the same time that he filled his own coffers and those of his authors. For he generously offered Sir Walter a share in the profits of the poems and novels he would include in this series. Sir Walter could furnish a new preface to each; and thus feel that he earned a part of what would come to him. There was no doubt in any one's mind that this Miscellany would indeed make a vast fortune.

So Constable and Scott might both feel that with care they would ride this storm, and embark on new sailings on uncharted seas.

Sir Walter reflected on his resources; if this financial flurry in the London market should actually involve trouble for Constable, which meant trouble for James Ballantyne and Company, which meant Walter Scott, the monied partner, why then, what could he count upon ? He cast up his accounts and thanked God that his circumstances were good; he would at this very time be able with his resources to pay more than pound for pound. "But" he recorded devoutly, "the sun and moon shall dance on the green ere carelessness, or hope of gain, or facility of getting cash, shall make me go too deep again, were it but for the disquiet of the thing."

If the worst came, however, it would not be all bad; he would gain an immense amount of time, being freed of the obligations of rich man; he would not play host to all Scotland and England; a stout resolution, for he had really been bored less than any man he knew; he had found some value in the company of even tiresome people; he had rarely met any one from whom he had not extracted either amusement or edification. Still he would stop this lavish hospitality; he was not well; he would enjoy quiet and leisurely writing without fear of constant interruption. He would tell the Caliph himself that he was not at home.

New rumors made disaster inevitable; sorrowfully Sir Walter walked about Abbotsford, these halls he had built, these woods and gardens he had created. He had, he supposed, been rash in anticipating funds in order to buy land, a hill here, a wood there, a mile of fair land along the Tweed; but then his prospects had always been enormous since the publication of his first poem. He would not want to remain with a diminished crest, live a poor man where he had been romantically wealthy. But half an hour after he had reconciled himself to the worst, assuring Charlotte who clung to hopes, that no miracle could save them, Cadell, Constable's partner, the cautious man of the concern, came with the latest letter from London, saying that Hurst and Robinson had so far stood the storm. A day later and Constable's confidence seemed safe to trust, Constable's cleverness would see them all through the crisis. Constable was far from being well, but his mind was active with schemes to help. He would start an expensive edition of the Waverley Novels, a guinea a volume. He was sure they would sell rapidly and make a mint of money; of course Scott should have a share of the profits. Write the prefaces of these, he urged, write at once, and we'll begin. Constable was irritable enough with Cadell; but otherwise steady enough, and fertile in suggestions. They could all enjoy their Christmas with light hearts.

But on Christmas Sir Walter's joy was interrupted by his sharp illness. Lady Scott forgot all this nonsense

SIR WALTER SCOTT'S STUDY AT ABBOTSFORD

THE ENTRANCE HALL AT ABBOTSFORD

about money difficulties in her solicitude over her dear Scott. She hovered by his bed, smoothing his pillow, administering draughts, sympathetic over pain, happy when it was finally relieved. She knew how to make a patient comfortable; she was deft and gentle and quiet. His dear Charlotte. She had never overvalued wealth; as each increase had come she had taken it calmly. She had not worried over money matters from the start. Whatever they had had she had lived within their income, not counting pennies, but somehow adjusting her expenditure within the margin of comfort. She had taken great pleasure in the fittings of Abbotsford; but no greater than that she had had in the humbler fittings of Lasswade. As she had grown older she had, to be sure, valued gaiety less; she did not care to roam much from the comforts of her own fireside. Her happiness had rested in her family. She had always expected him to be rich; she had taken his accession of wealth calmly. She did not believe that they would lose their fortune; if they did she would bear up like the sensible woman she was.

But he was glad that her fortitude would not be called upon. As he lay in bed thankful for the relief from his torture, weakened by the liberal lettings of blood believed curative by his physicians, he thought over the past. How little of pain it had held, how much of happiness ! He could think of no enemies and of many friends. In all his writings he had not hurt a single person, he thought; certainly he had never meant to. Few authors could claim as much. He had ever deprecated a sarcastic tongue. Lockhart, now, had almost spoiled his chances of advancement with the silly satirical publications of his youth. Anne was a bit inclined to satire; he must admonish her. And his nephew Walter occasionally let his tongue run away with him. He was young, but not too young to learn prudence; he was fatherless; and here his uncle had come near to ruin; he must do nothing that would injure his prospects.

On the whole this illness was a relief; he had been worried over absurdities lately; his pen had not always said what he meant it to; he repeated himself; he wrote the wrong words; nay in speaking he had sometimes of late been troubled for the right word. It was partly worry, and partly illness; this attack had been brewing. He was thankful it hadn't been paralysis as he had feared, the disease that had attacked his father and brother and that might make short shrift of him. He had had one slight stroke of apoplexy; *St. Ronan's Well* had been writing then, and had shown the effects of it. Well he didn't want that; and he didn't like to feel that he might be losing his mind. These slips had been merely temporary; he had been sickening; he had been worrying.

The New Year came in with good news; in a week affairs would be completely straightened. To answer James Ballantyne's demand for money to tide over, he would raise ten thousand pounds on the estate; when he had settled the estate on Walter the agreement had been that he could burden it to the extent of ten thousand pounds for the benefit of the younger children, Anne and Charles. Here was a greater need. He signed a bond and handed the money over to Ballantyne. Prudence would see them safely out of this sea of troubled waters. From London came reports of many a wealthy person impoverished over night. Ballantyne, however, saw the immediate ending of all their fears.

A week later a mysteriously worded letter from Constable awoke anew the sense of danger. Constable had supposedly gone to London two weeks since to arrange for the sale of some of his immense stock and thus raise money to tide affairs over. He had instead dallied in Scotland, keeping himself out of sight, and doing nothing. This was provoking; still one must have patience. The letter sounded ill; it seemed to be worded so that it told no disaster and yet let disaster be inferred. James Ballantyne, however, thought his interpretation wrong. James had faith in Constable's ability to raise money enough.

Three days later Ballantyne admitted that hope was gone, giving way completely to gloom. Sir Walter refused to be despondent. After all it was better to have the blow descend than to have the sword dangling over one's head. Charlotte and Anne were sufficiently depressed; but they were both patient. Anne, after all, was young; and she might yet marry. Her tale was not all told. As for Charlotte she had never failed him yet; she would not now. She was not one whose happiness depended upon material splendors. And they could never be really poor while he had his pen.

As for himself he had always loved being a bear and sucking his paws in solitude; that was preferable to being a lion and ramping for the amusement of others. Truly the blowing off of his hat on a stormy day had been often a cause of greater uneasiness than this seeming calamity. So long as his wife and daughter could look cheerily forward to reduced circumstances he would not grieve. "Ill luck, that direful chemist, never put into his crucible a more indissoluble piece of stuff" than Sir Walter Scott. He had sat at the feast of Fortune until he was fair satiated. He could not believe that Fortune's finger could play a dirge on him for more than a brief period; it never had before. He would go out into his grounds and plant three acorns as symbols of his luck; if they grew fast he would know that he would discharge his debts with equal rapidity. He would write his finger-ends off before he would give up Abbotsford and let strange feet claim its paths. He had on hand a novel all but done, considering the speed with which he composed; he had his *Life of Napoleon* well on its way. He had in his brain the making of dozens of books. He would not go bankrupt, no, not he; he would not give up his life-interest in Abbotsford. He would explain to the creditors that if they would but leave him Abbotsford and his income he would redouble his energies; he would write as he had never written before. And no man could say that Sir Walter Scott's pen had been lazy or unremunerative. No matter what his obligations were, he would warrant that he could clear them off. Suppose it took him two years, three years, what then ? He was not old yet; he was not worn out. Give him his health and Abbotsford and he would show his powers. The only lottery to which he would look was the public favor. That might not last;

but it had been his for twenty years; it might last another decade. He was not frightened at work; indeed as he looked back over the years he knew well that part of the very happiness had been his heavy work. He liked work; he liked to be busy. He would push forward this novel, *Woodstock,* as fast as ever he had written his poetry. It was a relief to bury himself in romance, in the doings of fanciful characters, and thus turn his mind from the painful thoughts of his own affairs.

Even Charlotte did not pity him; she had grown too long accustomed to his success. She leaned on him as she had from the very first when she came a bride without friends in Edinburgh. He had surrounded her with friends, with life of the gaiest. He had made her happy as she had made him. Well, he did not want pity; it was weak of him to have felt for a moment that she should sympathize with his troubles; the point was that she did not admit the possibility of trouble while he was there to protect her. To be sure they would be, for them, in straitened circumstances for a time; but he would pull them up; they should yet resume their splendid way of living. Only give him time . . .

The amount of the debts was appalling beyond his worst fears. The total liabilities of the three firms came to over half a million pounds; and of these nearly one hundred and twenty thousand were the share of James Ballantyne and Company, printers; James Ballantyne and *Company;* and "Company," meaning Sir Walter Scott, had to shoulder it all. He had been a fool, perhaps; Lockhart for all his kindness intimated as much. Poor

Charlotte could never find it in her heart to blame her husband for anything. As usual she poured out her wrath on the others. Her Scott had been too trusting; he had relied on Ballantyne and on Constable and they had betrayed his trust. Lockhart, while he had the strongest feelings of reproach for Ballantyne, could not conceal his wonder that the great Sir Walter had sullied his hands with trade.

Of course it would be simple to throw all the blame on James; Lockhart was no doubt right that James had been but a negligent bookkeeper. He had sensed that himself ten years ago when James was sitting like a gentleman in his parlor revising Scott's hasty manuscripts and reading proof. John had been alive then, merry little John; he had busied himself with that unlucky publishing venture — and yet it had not been so unlucky in the end; they had after all got rid of every last book. But he, Sir Walter, had seen that not even a printing business with its presses engaged to the limit of capacity could run itself without some one on the premises; he had told the brothers that one of them would have to have his office in the quarters of the Canongate Press. So James had taken a cubicle where he sat with the manuscripts. Perhaps Lockhart was right; perhaps he hadn't balanced his accounts or supervised the presses; he had not seen to such things as repair and replacement; he had never audited the accounts. He, Sir Walter, had from the beginning pleaded for simplicity in bookkeeping; he had originally intended to go over the books himself regularly. But he had been too busy creating

books for the presses to print to tend to these affairs.
Perhaps he, too, had been negligent.  Lockhart said that
James had taken out too much money; James said that
he had, according to the supposed rule of the printing
business, paid himself fifty pounds for every fifty pounds
paid in wages.  He had been entitled to his dreams of
prosperity, too.  Anyhow there was no use crying over
spilt milk.

He himself had been much younger when he had
entered into this business; he had had a growing family;
he had seen others get rich by his pen; he had seen an
opportunity to enlarge his income.  He had given up
hopes of prospering through a career as a practicing lawyer; his only hold on the legal profession was his clerkship and his sheriffdom.  As sheriff he drew a paltry
three hundred pounds a year; as clerk he had expected to
draw thirteen hundred.  Unfortunately the holder of the
clerkship who had resigned it to him, had been entitled to
the income for life; so that Scott for many years had
merely the labor without any compensation whatsoever.
No one could have expected the old man to live on and
on; but he did and the income had been in abeyance.
Charlotte's income of five hundred a year had seemed a
great deal to him when they had married; it became a
mere trifle as their expenses had mounted.  He could not
see but that he was justified in having caught at a simple
way of adding to his profits from his writings which were
the mainstay of their existence.  Even he had had no
suspicion of the enormous popularity of his verse and
prose.  He had thought the thousand pounds paid for

*Marmion* was princely. So it was then; now it was a pitiful sum compared to what anything he wrote brought.

As for pulling out of the partnership, there had never seemed to be any reason for doing so, and if he had James would have been seriously embarrassed; he would have had to hunt around for a monied partner, since he himself had never been able to bring capital to the concern. John had said that one of the reasons for the failure of the publishing house was that the funds were constantly taken for the printing establishment; maybe he was right; but he had made a mess of things much more quickly than James.

It was useless to ruminate on the how and whys. The fiasco had come and must be faced. Sir Walter dreaded his first day at court whither as clerk he must go. He felt like the man with a large nose, he reflected; he was sure that all the world would stare at him. The Great Unknown had alas! become the Little Known. Yet it had been a satisfaction to tell the creditors that he was the author of the Waverley Novels and as such able to promise them huge sums each year in payment. Constable had not been very happy when he learned that Sir Walter did not consider the works in preparation his. Constable, poor wretch, was worse off than he; Constable had no vein of fairy gold to tap; he had no steady income; he had had to sell valuable copyrights at a sacrifice; he was reduced to a tiny shop, he who had been prince of booksellers. Sir Walter had, after all, a sure income; his clerkship had finally fallen in, there was his

SIR WALTER SCOTT
*From a painting by Sir Henry Raeburn*

sheriffdom, and Charlotte's pittance. His creditors might have seized upon his income; they might have completely beggared him; and then his spirit would indeed have been crushed. He doubted if he could ever have written a line again. But he was to have his income and his freedom to spin tales that would pay all. No sum was impossible so long as he had hours to sit at his desk and weave romances; indeed in some ways the misfortune was fortune; for now that he ceased to keep open house for all the world, he had hours given back to him, hours in which he could write.

For the creditors had been most kind. There had, indeed, at one time, been an attempt to set aside the settlement of Abbotsford upon Walter. Then the estate could have been sold, with all its trappings and fittings; of course if the creditors chose they could at once order the furniture, books, and antiquities sold. But if they tried to wrest Abbotsford from his son, then he would fight. He knew law himself. He would sell everything he could to pay the costs of a lawsuit that would, he knew, be bitterly expensive. But he would not give up Abbotsford. He had according to the marriage agreement settled it upon his son. He was not trying to cheat his creditors; they were safe enough if they would only give him time. He was not asking them to take the pitiful settlement of Constable and of Hurst and Robinson; he would pay pound for pound, not like them, a shilling or two to the pound. Granted that his popularity lasted he would pay all; in five brief years these present difficulties would be a joke. If the creditors persisted in this plan to ruin him they would be killing the goose that laid the golden egg.

The creditors were canny Scotchmen; they were shrewd men and shrewd bankers. Moreover they were all of them well disposed toward the man who had brought renown to Scotch letters; the man who had made Scotland a Mecca for tourists not only from all Britain but from America and the continent. He had, as it were, played prince of Scotland; his home had been the centre of hospitality; he had represented Scotland to the outside world. Such a man was not to be disgraced; was not to be pushed hard.

At the very first rumor of disaster the banks had offered to lend him money; prudently he had refused. If Hurst and Robinson were to fail, it were best to have the event over; there was little use in prolonging a difficult situation. The directors of the Royal Bank, however, wished him to know that they were ready to help him in any way possible. Sir William Forbes came personally to see him, to offer help in the kindest way though his bank was one of the heaviest creditors; Sir William Forbes, kind-hearted gentleman. In their youth how they two had glared at each other ! How they had quarreled ! How they had almost fought duels for the privilege of turning the pages of Williamina Stuart's music ! They had not met often since then. Sir William had won Williamina; had taken her to his country estate where she had borne him a large family and then had died at a time when he, Scott, who had been too impecunious a suitor, had been in the first heyday of his magnificent success. She had lived to see him win a position which Sir William's wealth could never buy; and to see his wealth surpass anything she had ever known or dreamt of. Well, that wealth was a shadow now. But once again the shadow would become substance, if only his popularity held out. He must make haste with the books on hand. He must test his fate.

The creditors had appointed a board of trustees who gave him time, which was all he needed. Daily there came to him offers of substantial help. Jane, dear little thing, had written post haste to offer her entire fortune to her father-in-law. Bless her heart ! he wouldn't beggar her and Walter. He would pull out of this mire by his own exertions.

Even more touching was the visit of the music master who had taught Sophia and Anne the harp; the little man pressed upon him the entire savings of his life, five or six hundred pounds which to him was a fortune. Equally gratifying was an anonymous offer of thirty thousand pounds; but even this his pride could not accept. Walter Scott alone would pay the debts for which Walter Scott was liable.

More mirth-provoking was the offer of a patent medicine man who had perceived the possibilities of advertising. He was a man born out of his century. His scheme seemed merely ludicrous to his contemporaries. His suggestion was that Sir Walter endorse his remedy which the public would then buy, and he would split the profits. Sir Walter was not ready to become the world's pioneer endorser.

He would put his nose to the grindstone and make money honestly. James was all right; he had had to give up his grand house and take to simpler quarters; but his family was comfortable. He still had the editing of his *Weekly Journal;* and he could still work at the printing press; which, as soon as the trustees began to run it, began immediately to show a profit, at the rate of some twelve hundred pounds a year. He had, then, been right in thinking it a paying concern. As for Constable, he must manage his own affairs. Cadell had split with him; and on the whole it would be better to deal with Cadell. Constable without Cadell was like a clock without a pendulum. Cadell was the shrewder business man; and he, Scott, could not afford to take chances. Everything he published now must be well managed, must be a success. There was no room for failures. Honest James had been frightfully perturbed when he had written nonsense those first worried days. There would be no more nonsense.

# CHAPTER VII

*And long ere dinner time, I have*
*Full eight close pages wrote;*
*What, Duty, hast thou now to crave?*
*Well done, Sir Walter Scott!*

— WALTER SCOTT.

## CHAPTER VII

IT WAS with resolution that Sir Walter at fifty-five set about the rearrangement of his life. After all it was silly to practise petty economies; he would resume his cigars; Charlotte need not worry needlessly; her regular fortnightly allowance of twenty-four pounds would continue. He might be pinched; he was, alas, head over ears in debt; but they were far from being penniless. The first thing to do was to reduce to one establishment, Abbotsford. The dear old Edinburgh house, 39 Castle Street, must go. No need now to keep two staffs of servants; his attendance in town was only a third of the year; and even then he would as before have the long week-end at Abbotsford — court did not sit on Mondays. He would take a simple lodging where he would require only a body servant. He would give up keeping a carriage in town; he had always preferred to walk anyhow. There would be no sense in giving up the horses and carriages at Abbotsford; their sale would bring little; and their upkeep was slight. They would move to Abbotsford the books of 39 Castle Street, and such of the furniture as they cared for. The rest would have to be sold. What a task this would have been for John Ballantyne, to auction off the possessions of the Great Unknown !

Well, there would be one advantage: they would at

last get rid of a mess of paltry things, expensive enough to be sure, but ugly in proportion to their would-be elegance, the gifts of unknown admirers. He had paid for them in torturing the English language to make his thanks more or less sincere. What would the public say about those frightful paintings, such numbers of them, too! He couldn't label them, could he, "gifts of a vain old lady?"

Charlotte, equally unwilling to wear her heart on her sleeve, laughed at his jokes; and went busily about among their possessions, choosing what she could not part with. Sir Walter noticed with a pang that she passed over many a relic of their early days. He himself, for all his resolute determination, could not see these things go into the hands of strangers. He gave things away with a generous hand; this cabinet had been his father's; that picture had come from an uncle; this trinket was once an aunt's. And in the end the wagon was piled high with goods to be taken to Abbotsford.

There for days he was busy once more with carpenters; new shelves to be put up; old pictures to hang, stacks and stacks of books to arrange. Lady Scott lingered in the Edinburgh house, paying a final farewell to the rest of their familiar old furniture. He himself had been glad to get the wrench of parting over. He was never one to look back; the future beckoned.

He could not remember that he was poor when requests came in to him. His hand went to his pocket again and again to come up with a stray guinea or two. He subscribed for eighteen copies of an obscure starveling's book; he gave a dinner party now and then. There was still champagne to be had. He could still play the patron; he could still aid the editor of a struggling new paper with the gift of an article for which he could have received a hundred pounds or so. He could still aid an old friend, one who had made a pitiable failure of life, by permitting him to publish two sermons he had once written for his use. Life was not over yet !

So long as Abbotsford remained a family residence and gave up its pretentions to being a hall of welcome for all the world there was a plentiful staff of servants with those brought out from Edinburgh; Charlotte would not find housekeeping any more of a burden; indeed, rather less, since no longer would she be called upon to feed dukes and foreign princes at short notice. The housekeeper would bother her less; would be able to manage things herself without disturbing her mistress.

Anne would find life dull, he feared; for a time he would be unable to take her off on journeys. Charlotte had become such a stay-at-home that she would not mind; and she would be glad to have her restless husband always with her. And Sophia was off to London, Walter still in Ireland; Charles would, of course, remain at Oxford until he got his degree. Then there would be a position for him somewhere in the foreign office; his Majesty had promised that. The King had indeed been most sympathetic over the financial fiasco.

The whole world had been sympathetic. Damn it ! he didn't want sympathy. He'd put an end to this poor-manning in short order. With all the vim of his youth he turned to a task that would divert the public mind from his calamity. He tossed off his *Malachi* letters which came to the defence of the Scottish banks and their dearly prized privilege of issuing pound notes. The general disorder of the London financial market which had brought about the ruin of Hurst and Robinson to cause his indebtedness had produced a stringent bill in Parliament. The privileges of banks throughout the realm should be curtailed; had the banks not lent money right and left on the flimsiest securities the panic could not have occurred. The bankers of Scotland were wroth; they refused to be classed with their English brethren; they insisted upon issuing banknotes. The letters of *Malachi* sprang to the defence of the Scottish privileges.

No sooner were they published in the *Quarterly* than they were quoted on every tongue; they were praised; they were reviled; they were everything but ignored. There was a call for an issue of them in pamphlet form; James Ballantyne quickly struck off an edition. All the world was arguing about Sir Walter Scott's *Malachi;* and Sir Walter Scott's debt was forgotten. The House of Commons spent a stormy session over *Malachi.* Here was incitement to sedition ! In a harsher day such a writer would have paid the penalty of treason for this. Defenders of Scott sprang up. Revilers and defenders alike united to call him the mightiest magician of his age, a man whose views were entitled to respect. In the end the troublesome bill was defeated and the bankers of Scotland rested triumphant.

This somewhat relieved the gloom that had settled

SIR WALTER SCOTT
*From an original painting*

upon Sir Walter over the removal from Castle Street,
when he ceased to be a householder in Edinburgh as his
father had been sixty years ago.   There was no use sitting
and glowering.   Out he went for a long walk.   When he
returned he needed no longer to argue with himself
whether it was body or mind, whether the fiddle or the
fiddlestick made the music.   It was obvious that it was
but the stick that played his mournful tune, his body
which cried aloud for exercise. Exercise and work, in
these two lay his salvation.

> I loll in my chair,
> And around me I stare
> With a critical air,
> Like a calf at a fair;
> And, say I, Mrs. Duty,
> Good-morrow to your beauty,
> I kiss your sweet shoe-tie,
> And hope I can suit ye.

Heavy days were, however, at hand, days in which
merry invocations to duty were of no avail.  Lady Scott
had been ailing for two years or more; but with her
reluctance to make her illness a subject for discussion she
had constantly understated her distresses even when she
could be brought to mention them at all.   Her husband
in spite of occasional forebodings believed her consti-
tution sufficiently vigorous to conquer this abominable
asthma.  Now she seemed visibly worse; he urged her
to see a physician, especially since they were to retire
to the country; at Abbotsford there would be no doctor
close at hand; she had best get advice while she was
in Edinburgh.  The physician recommended digitalis

which, upon her arrival at Abbotsford, she persisted in bravely though the nausea it induced was worse than the disease.

For weeks Sir Walter alternated between hope and fear. To add to his distress the news from London was dreary; Sophia, always inclined to valetudinarianism herself, reported ill health as her confinement approached; and little Johnie, the beautiful, witty, sweet-tempered little boy, the darling of the whole family, unspoiled in spite of the attentions showered upon him, this precocious and loveable child was despaired of. The little boy's spine was affected; at times he could not walk or even sit. Sophia had tried all the nostrums in the pharmacopeia; she had tried a doctor who professed to cure with care, not with drugs.

He remembered his own invalid childhood when his parents had carried him about to doctors. He could still visualize the establishment where he had seen earls wound round with electrical contraptions, collars, and belts of magnets rivalling those of Indian chiefs. He remembered well this Temple of Health whither people had flocked partly to be cured, partly to admire the elaborately adorned hall, a dazzle of color and crystal, partly to see if it were true that Lady Hamilton (whom rakish young men referred to as that "celebrated *fille de joie*") was really posing as the Goddess of Health. The young Walter Scott had had his electrical treatments as well as the vaunted earth bath but he had not been present at the brawl during which a young man had been killed with a red-hot poker. After that episode the house had tumbled

literally about its proprietor's ears, the furious mob tear-
ing down the trumpery ornaments, and the magistrates
somewhat belatedly closing the establishment. The
learned doctor could no longer march down the aisle
of a fashionable church resplendent in his suit of silver
and white, his head topped with a mountainous wig.
When the magistrates refused to allow him to set up as
a lecturer he took revenge in a series of vigorous advertise-
ments which in bold print informed the delighted public
that he looked down upon the magistrates "as the sun
in his meridian glory looks down on the poor, feeble,
stinking glimmer of an expiring candle, or as G— himself, in the plenitude of his omnipotence, may regard the
insolent bouncings of a few refractory maggots in a rot-
ten cheese."

Little John Hugh Lockhart's doctors were less picturesque; one could hope that they were more sound.
Sophia's newest enthusiasm was apparently a physician
in good repute. Meanwhile she had now taken the child
to the seashore where he and she might both be benefited.
Her constant and devoted attendance on the sick child
might harm the one about to be born. Fortunately little
John gained a temporary respite, and the baby coming
into the world a little ahead of time was honored with
the name of Walter. Perhaps the name would be of
good omen; his grandfather reflected that it was a favorite
name in the family. His own parents had used it on
two sons before they had found one to live to bear it;
he himself had been their third Walter, their ninth child.
Six children had they lost before they had been able to

raise one.  Six children of their thirteen had they raised, and none now alive but he himself, he the lame invalid for whose life they had long despaired.  Perhaps little Johnie would recover and grow strong, too. Perhaps this latest Walter would bring new glory to the name.

It was well that Sir Walter did not live to watch the progress of this Walter Lockhart, that gay, thoughtless young man whose vices caused infinite pain to his father before death cut short his ill-starred career.  Had he been able to look into the future Sir Walter might have labored less hard to save his estates.  His own sons died without issue, and without having taken up residence at Abbotsford.  The great house was deserted until Sophia's daughter, turned Catholic with her husband under the influence of the Oxford movement, came to add a new wing with a Catholic chapel and make the place once more a home.

But at the time the birth of the boy Walter and the improvement in the health of the crippled child gave Sir Walter as much pleasure as he could feel while his wife, the dear companion of nearly thirty years, was drawing to the inevitable close of her life.  With deep sadness he removed to a cot in his dressing-room, forced to give up to an attendant his place in Charlotte's room.  He reflected gloomily that he might never return.  Again he assured himself that Charlotte could not fail to recover. When she was in sharp pain he could almost wish her relief in any form; but she was not always in pain.  He took his walks in loneliness and depression.  How he missed having Charlotte at his elbow !  Nothing looked quite the same without her; he wanted to turn to her every moment with his comments.

Back he hurried to the sickroom where his niece and his daughter, both of them Anne Scott, were in attendance. Charlotte was smiling. He leaned over her to catch her faint words: "You all have such melancholy faces!" He rushed from the room. This blow of misfortune was too heavy to be borne. Valiantly he wrestled with his own gloom; he would not give way whatever black fate was his. But it was hard to keep up his courage; the sight of Charlotte weak, suffering, dying would break his spirits. Business called him to Edinburgh; he would go; Charlotte slept for the most part, and the two Annes were always with her. They were fortunate, they could do something for the sufferer, they could make her comfortable, they could keep her room in that tidy order she loved. He could do nothing. Perhaps it was as well if she did not see his melancholy face; and yet how could he keep it cheerful?

He had been in town three days when Anne's sad letter reached him. Never before had he gone to Abbotsford with reluctance. Over and over there churned in his mind the words "gone — gone — for ever — ever — ever." What should he do with the major portion of his thoughts which had been hers for thirty years? They would be hers for a long time to come, do what he would. He could not alter the habit of a lifetime. He could not get over this cherishing of thoughts and anecdotes to share with her; he could not help looking up from his book to meet her sweet glance; only now she

was no longer there.   She had been so sweet, so kind and
courteous, so thoughtful of his comfort, so loving . . .
he fell asleep in his chair and heard her calling him.   She
had been asleep when he parted from her; he remembered his hope that she would wake refreshed. He had
told himself that there was no hope but he had not believed himself.   He *had* hoped; now there was no hope.
The bright May day was such as she had loved; gentle
weather as she was gentle.   He could not believe that
she was gone forever; he must and would see her again.
There must be another world where they would meet
free from mortal sorrows and frailties.   She must be
somewhere, sentient and conscious of his grief.   No prize
the world could offer could buy his belief that there was
a hope that he would be with her again; the how and the
where were uncertain, were mysterious; they were true
none the less.

It was no part of his philosophy to groan over grief;

> Since these things are necessities
> Then let us meet them like necessities.

That was well enough in its way; it was truth; yet it
was poor consolation.   It needed all his conscious stoi-
cism to carry him over the arrival of his sons, both
truly grieving, Walter, the only child she had nursed,
quite overcome.   Anne, poor girl, fell from one fainting
fit into another; she was worn out with her long watching and nursing as well as with sorrow.   He must set his
children an example of fortitude; he must set himself to
work to re-establish his fortune for their sakes, for the

sake of his own character; he must give himself no leisure to indulge in discouraging thoughts. And yet he must allow himself some luxury of grief. He forced himself to re-enter the bedroom where the impress of the coffin still remained on the coverlet; he forced himself to sleep in the bed they had occupied together. He slept ill, dreaming that she was beside him; in the long watches of the night never again would he have someone to turn to, someone to talk to.

The days were little relief to his feeling of solitude. In the evening he stole away to his study on a pretense of work, but really to relieve the two Annes of his gloomy presence. The room had never been so quiet, so oppressively silent. His Charlotte would have been in and out a dozen times by now; she would have come to see if the fire was burning brightly; if he had changed his damp shoes; if he had plenty of paper, or cigars, or what not. She would have had a hundred questions to ask: whether he wanted the carriage tomorrow morning or if she should arrange a drive for some guest; whether he had settled that incident which had been bothering him this morning; whether he wanted her to copy anything. He had got used to her interruptions; he actually could not work as fast without them. No longer could he look up from his papers to watch her fidget about the room, straightening a curtain, putting a chair in place, making neat his pile of reference books. Never again could he beguile the tedious twilight hour with one completely in sympathy with him. He almost felt her presence; it could not be true that she was gone, gone forever. In the bitter realization he fell into hysterical sobbing.

This would never do. He threw himself feverishly into *Napoleon;* he began to weave a romance as a relief from this heavy research. Overwork to some extent smothered regrets and grievings but it made his head ache, his eyes ache, his back ache; and most of all his heart ached. Was Duty not satisfied ?

He returned to Edinburgh, glad that legal business swallowed a part of the long days. He went to a committee meeting and was diverted by his fellowmen. On the way back to his lodgings he realized with a start that he could no longer talk these things over with Charlotte. She had been wont to listen to his news and look grave or laugh outright at his recital. With no Charlotte to astonish or amuse with these matters he found that no longer did they interest him.

Lodgings were not home. They were a mere protection from the cold and wet; he had rather walk the streets than sit in this ugly hole. Not so had Charlotte kept her rooms, untidy, unkempt, uninviting. He did not mind the food very much; he had been satiated with the rich table at Abbotsford; besides for years now he had again and again been restricted to simple diet. He could savor his broth and boiled beef like any humble Scotchman, though he could wish the worthy Mrs. Brown understood the art of cookery better. Charlotte would never have kept a cook of this stamp. And whatever the widow's virtues she was no judge of cheese. Somewhat shamefacedly he bought a bit of gruyère to add to his

supper. Alas, he thought, when had he before had to
buy food for his eating !

Well, in July he would get to Abbotsford again and
Anne would take care of him; when he returned to town
he would find a furnished house and bring Anne along;
it would be better for him and better for her; now she was
lonely in the country and he in the city. Since his
thoughts had become heavy his pen had become light.
He inscribed verses of farewell which would not have
complimented his landlady:

> So good-by, Mrs. Brown,
> I am going out of town,
> Over dale, over down,
> Where bugs bite not,
> Where lodgers fight not,
> Where below you chairmen drink not,
> Where beside you gutters stink not;
> But all is fresh, and clean, and gay,
> And merry lambkins sport and play. . .

That was over. Now he would have to face Abbotsford alone. He would not have it thought that there was
any way in which he could be beaten. The journey out
with no Charlotte beside him in the carriage had given
his thoughts a bilious tendency. He threw himself into
the unpacking of a case of books just returned from the
binder. He determined to take the two Annes on walks
and drives and resume his pleasant intercourse with his
neighbors. He accepted an invitation to stay overnight;
and was lodged in the room where he had been wont
to stay those many years ago when he was a young
bachelor. Now once more he was single. Then he had

looked forward with hope; now he looked back with regret. But he must not let vain repining make him worse than he was; this way madness lay.

He plunged headlong into work. Fortunately a crew of old friends descended upon Abbotsford, among them his actor protégé Terry, ill, despondent, unable to determine his future way of livelihood. Terry was worse off than he for all his comparative youth. He could give refuge to Terry's young son and supervise his education in Edinburgh. Terry could not successfully take care of himself and his wife. Terry had no projects to which he could set his hand.

This bothersome *Life of Napoleon* wasn't such a bad scheme; it was taking a confounded amount of research, more than enough for a dozen novels, but it kept him occupied and it would in the end richly repay the labor. It would take him away from Abbotsford for a time, for which he was sorry now that he had turned hermit. Yet it would do him good to go out into the world once more.

He would enjoy being with Sophia and Lockhart, he would enjoy telling Johnie tales to beguile the hours of sickness. He remembered his own petted childhood, when he had been the idol of his grandparents and all the servants of the farm. He wondered if Johnie would suffer when the baby, the newest Walter, grew old enough to tease him. He himself had suffered horribly when he first came in contact with his brothers. At the farm he had been king. When at seven or eight he had gone back to his father's house he had found life hard. His brothers had not yielded to him in the least; they had snatched his toys, torn his books, laughed at his romantic notions. When he got in their way they politely knocked him down. When he opposed them they kicked with even better aim. He remembered now his utter rage and astonishment that he should be so treated, he the little lame prince. And his sister had had far more attention than he, she who was always unlucky, always getting into some painful scrape, squashing her hand in the iron gate, setting fire to her cap, falling into the stone pit. Johnie's delicate health could have dispensed with a brother. And yet a child who almost surely could not live to maturity was a slender hope for parents to cling to. He himself had felt that Sophia needed other children.

He would soon be with them. He had to go to London to examine Napoleon's correspondence from St. Helena. How bitter he used to be against the fellow; he had thought him lucky to be allowed to breathe the air even of a desert island. And yet in earlier days he had not felt so; he had been grateful to the chap for bringing a jolly war into the world. How he had enjoyed his military prancings! He and his fellows had revelled in their voluntary troop; they had fancied themselves the defenders of their country. They had been disappointed enough when Napoleon failed to invade either England or Scotland. And now here he was working over the fellow's life, forcing himself to the task blithely begun, in order to pay huge debts that were not of his making. The Great Unknown had come to his Waterloo; but no,

he hadn't.   He would work harder and faster; he would
not be beaten.   He would pay his debts and enlarge Abbotsford yet.

His determination increased when he heard that a firm
of money-lenders holding some two thousand pounds of
bills for which he was responsible threatened to make
trouble if he came to London.   What did the wretches
think ? that they could clap him in jail for debt ?   What
nonsense.   Such discourteous people deserved no consideration.   He had announced his intention of paying
every last shilling; he was not one to compound his debts;
no paltry settlement for him.   So if they chose to force
his hand they would themselves be the losers.   He would
take refuge in the Isle of Man and they could whistle
for their money until he was ready.   His other creditors
were men of sense; they realized that their best hope lay
in leaving him his income so that he might live decently
and turn his time to good account.   These Ahabs would
strip him.

He never knew that the Ahabs' power was drawn from
them by Sir William Forbes, Williamina's widowed husband.   Sir William quietly bought up the bill and added
it to those held by his own bank, waiting Sir Walter's
good time to discharge it.

All Sir Walter knew was that he was free to come and
go as he chose.   Down to London he travelled in comfort, his daughter at his side.   A little change, a little
gaiety would do Anne good.   Her spirits had been sadly
crushed by her mother's death following so soon upon
her father's disaster.   She would brighten up in London.

Like her mother she had been softened by prosperity; it had been hard for her to face adversity. She was young; London would divert her. It was a pity the ten thousand five hundred guineas Longman had already offered for his *Napoleon* could not even buy her a bauble or two. He himself got sufficient pleasure out of the offer because it demonstrated his essential soundness to his creditors; it showed his value in the literary market. A man who could sell his efforts at such prices — and *Woodstock* had brought in eight thousand pounds — would not take long to settle every account that could possibly be held against him.

Anne was surprised and delighted to have her father summoned to Windsor immediately upon his arrival in London. His Majesty was pleased to give Sir Walter a whole day of his time; he made him sit beside him and he listened to him with interest and courtesy. His Majesty talked well himself, too. Altogether it was a pleasant day; only it was less of a pleasure to talk it over with Anne than it had been with Charlotte. Anne had her share of fun too; every day they dined out or had people in to dine with them; Anne met lords and ladies, dukes, earls, marchionesses, actors, painters, journalists, poets. It was a crowded week before they set out for Paris to consult Napoleon material there. At Paris Anne was delighted with the theatres. At the Odeon *Ivanhoe* was playing as an opera. Sir Walter saw it with mingled feelings. How ill he had been when he had dictated those words which now came trippingly from the hero's tongue! He could feel the griping pains in his stomach yet. He had been ready to believe then that he would never live to finish that novel.

His friends had thought that he would be lionized in France; he was thankful that he did not expect anything of the sort. He was sensible enough not to overvalue public praise; as a literary man he had to reckon with public applause; as a private gentleman he had always found popular clamor embarrassing. The breath which made shouts for him today might make them against him tomorrow. He would probably be quite unknown in France.

Whether he valued adulation or not, it knocked at his door before three days were out. Russian princesses, the American author Fenimore Cooper, ambassadors, portrait painters, authors, journalists, lion hunters, all came to stare or to talk. His portrait had to be painted, his autograph signed. Letters poured in upon him. A gallant Frenchman threatened to hang himself if the great Sir Walter would not immediately transfer himself to the writer's home. Sir Walter invited Cooper to breakfast but hardly had the two authors got well into a discussion of copyright laws, without having time to enter into Cooper's suggestion of American editions of the Waverley Novels, when in bounced voluble Frenchmen in twos and threes, exploding compliments. Conversation became impossible; the two authors yielded to importunity and sat side by side to have their portraits painted.

Sir Walter took Anne out to see the King go to chapel. His Majesty recognized him and stepped out of his path to greet the famous author. The ladies of the royal family bowed graciously. Anne, unused to royalty, was overcome at the distinction conferred upon them. Her father could estimate properly this favor as well as the public adulation. Pleasant as it was it was transitory. His reputation might last a generation after him, perhaps two generations; it was not of the deathless variety. He was glad he did not overvalue himself or this literature of his making. This Bow-wow strain he could manage with the best of them; and it suited the public taste apparently; if it didn't how could he ever have faced the world with a debt of over a hundred thousand pounds ? he a lawyer without a practice, a sheriff with a paltry three hundred a year, a clerk with a moderate thirteen hundred. What wealth he would have thought that clerkship once ! when Charlotte's five hundred had seemed princely.

He had not kept Charlotte waiting long for her carriage; he was glad to think of that; prosperity had come with his first literary scheme and had continued unbroken; he had always meant to use literature as a crutch, not as a staff; perhaps he had leaned too heavily upon its promises. He must lean on them still, however; they were his only hope against this heavy weight of debt.

The journey was proving expensive; it had cost fifty pounds just to carry him and Anne to London; how he would have laughed at a thought of fifty pounds a few short months ago ! It would be money well invested, however, because he had, both through his investigation of documents and through his contact with French people and places, come to have a firmer picture of Napo-

leon. Moreover he had cleared his mind of its gloomy
ideas. This seeing new scenes, this revisiting of familiar
places had driven the cobwebs from his brain. His
thoughts would run the clearer and faster.

In London once more he chatted gaily with Sir
Thomas Lawrence as he sat for the portrait commanded
by the king. He felt that Sir Thomas was making quite
a picture of his weatherbeaten old block, of the "stout
blunt carle who cared for few things and feared nothing."
Once upon a time he had been what men call handsome
in spite of his peaked dome; Charlotte hadn't quite liked
it when the children began to call him Peveril of the
Peak; but when she saw that he didn't mind she had
sometimes spoken of him herself as Peveril. The Sheriff,
the neighbors always said; the Shirra, the good Scotch
servants. He liked honest Tom Purdie's affectionate
Shirra ten times better than all this Sir Waltering. Tom
never used the title, no, not he; yet he had been mightily
pleased with its bestowal upon his master. The Shirra
laughed as he told his London friends how the old man
had worked a whole day to prefix an S to the W S
branded on the Abbotsford sheep, S W S, *Sir* Walter
Scott.

The sirring was laid on like axle grease here in London.
He was surfeited with compliments. And yet he had
felt uncommonly pleased when the gentle old lady who
had been Fanny Burney told him that she had been impatient to meet only two people, the statesman George
Canning and the poet Sir Walter Scott.

Though his pride was not, he hoped, unduly raised by

the flattering reception accorded him on two continents he felt his confidence in himself increased; his resolution strengthened. The extravagance of the trip would yet be on the credit side of the ledger; and he was too old a man to travel stingily. At Oxford he visited his son Charles, giving him the assurances of his friends in London that there would be a place in the foreign office. Even the sages here paid him homage.

But he must get home; this dragging a daughter and a train of servants about had cost him two hundred pounds. It was sad to reflect on expenses instead of upon experiences. He must attend strictly to duty now and bring himself back to the point where he need not count money.

It was not easy to push himself, however. Court was sitting, and the hours in the overheated rooms tired him more and more. He slept ill at night, and was disinclined to rise in the morning; in the old days had he felt like this he would have lolled in bed with soft hands caressing his brow, smoothing his pillow. Now he dragged himself, though late, out of bed and listened dully to the proceedings of the court. His head ached, his heart annoyed him with flutterings, his blood fairly churned in his veins. When old age came, sicknesses settled upon one thicker and thicker; fortunately the long halt would come at last and cure all.

Meanwhile he must whip himself to his heavy tasks. He would never see threescore and ten; he would be summed up at a discount. All the more reason for getting done as much as he could in the few years left to him. This rheumatism was most troublesome; he could hardly hobble about to get his books and maps but must be ringing all the time for a servant. He was an unseaworthy old hulk; he navigated with difficulty. He must have a bed brought downstairs to save his weary old legs. There was one advantage to all this blistering and bleeding, aside from the relief to pain—they took all the energy out of him and he felt no inclination to wander outdoors away from the insistent voice of duty. *Napoleon* would be the quicker done because of this illness.

*Napoleon* went ahead, with magazine articles sandwiched in between his battles. The rheumatism went on, too, yielding to sunny weather, doubling in the frost and cold. The ladies who so importunely proposed to him did not realize what a lame duck he was; maybe they thought he was a dashing old fellow. They'd never have a chance to know; he'd listen to no proposals. He ought to be flattered to have ladies of title and fortune eager to become Lady Scott; he wasn't; he had made his Charlotte Lady Scott; there would be no one to displace her.

But if people could constantly approach him with offers of marriage he could hardly consider himself forgotten. And here was William Murray, manager of the Edinburgh Theater, urging him to be chairman at the dinner given for the benefit of disabled actors. Three hundred tickets had been sold. It was the first really public affair to which he had been since his disaster. It would perhaps be as well to go; the world had stopped poor-manning him since those *Malachi* letters.

The dinner ran smoothly until Lord Meadowbank offered the first toast: "the health . . . of a great and distinguished individual, whose name must always stand by itself, and which . . . must ever be received, I will not say with ordinary feelings of pleasure or of delight, but with those of rapture and enthusiasm . . . the Great Unknown — the minstrel of our native land . . . we owe to him, as a people, a large and heavy debt of gratitude. . . It is to him that we owe our gallant ancestors and illustrious patriots . . . it is *He* who has called down upon their struggles for glory and freedom the admiration of foreign lands. He it is who has conferred a new reputation on our national character, and bestowed on Scotland an imperishable name, were it only by her having given birth to himself. I propose the health of Sir Walter Scott."

The final words were received with a roar. Long before his lordship had come to the middle of his speech men were standing on chairs and tables, waving their napkins, holding their glasses aloft. The enthusiasm was so wild that men forgot to drink. The hall rang with vocal applause. If Sir Walter had had any doubts of the place he held in the hearts of his fellow citizens this scene would have dispelled them. The public announcement of his identity with the Great Unknown created a sensation; he had for years been suspected of the authorship of the Waverley Novels; he had communicated the fact to his creditors. But only his creditors and the twenty trusted friends who had been in the secret from the first had been really aware; others suspected or they doubted; they did not know.

Next day all Edinburgh could talk of nothing else. It even created a stir below stairs. Soon the town was chuckling over the anecdote of the lady's maid who asked a companion who did write Shakespeare anyhow. "Oh," said her friend who worked for an actress, " 'twas Ben Jonson."

But there was a handy man about to correct such misinformation. "Wrong, both o' ye. It's Sir Walter Scott. He confessed it himsel' at a public dinner three days since."

Such triumphs might not be worth much in themselves; they did bolster up an aging man's spirits. More stimulating than any amount of praise was the solid accomplishment of reducing his debt in a year and a half by the goodly sum of twenty-eight thousand pounds. Before two years were out the debt had been cut by forty thousand pounds. Already his creditors had received more shillings to the pound of the total debt than Constable's and Hurst and Robinson's put together. Here was something to bolster up his pride; here was solid achievement. He had felt pleased when his countrymen toasted him as the singer of his ancestors' glory; he had felt elated when his creditors gave him a vote of confidence.

Not to fail in a task assumed, that was matter for pride; not to die with his name smirched by debt, that was worth the struggle, that was glory.

On the whole life was treating him pleasantly once more; when he tried to buy back his copyrights he had appealed to Murray who owned one-fourth part of *Marmion*. Cadell had approached Murray to find him adamant in his refusal. To Sir Walter's request Murray had replied like the gentleman he was: no amount of money could buy the copyright from him; he could not weigh gold against the honor of being the publisher even in small measure of Sir Walter Scott; but he had already reaped golden profits from his share in *Marmion;* he would feel honored if Sir Walter would accept his rights in it as his own.

Now the copyrights were all assembled — Cadell had paid out eighty-five hundred pounds for them for himself and Sir Walter and in the future they would divide the profits, Sir Walter's share going, of course to diminish his debts. Now he could with free heart refuse the various editorships offered him, those of two thousand pounds a year as easily as the less magnificent ones. With his new works and the profits from the old ones he would soon be abreast of the world.

To add to his pleasure his little grandson showed signs of improvement. He came to Abbotsford and once more rode his diminutive steed. The place was besieged with sightseers again. In France a Russian princess had told him that she would cross seas just for the sight of Sir Walter Scott. Many of these tourists seemed actually to have done so, if one could trust the superlatives of these Americans. In the good old days he would have dined and wined them; he would have put up half England, and what looked like all America, in his spare bed-rooms. Now he let them stare and go. On the whole it was pleasanter this way. He had no longer the zest for strangers.

With his debts well started on the downgrade, with his children and grandchildren about him, with the world's praise — though he recognized its hollowness — perpetually in his ears he began to feel that the present still had much to offer, the future something, too.

# CHAPTER VIII

*A most composed invincible man; . . . Samson-like,
carrying off on his strong Samson-shoulders the gates
that would imprison him. . .*

— Carlyle of Scott.

# CHAPTER VIII

THERE had been of late no lack of amusements though he did not join the two Annes in their excursions to the theatre or in their attendance at many a ball and merry-making. He had been little of a hermit with dinners at home and abroad, and pleasant public dinners or meetings. Old friends came once more to Abbotsford, the big house offering its wide hospitality. The world could hardly be regarding him as a ruined man or his mail would not be filled with begging letters. Not satisfied with writing (and making him pay a pretty sum in postage) these literary beggars travelled to his door which, after all, he could hardly slam in their faces. Again and again his hand went into his pocket to come up with anything between one and fifty guineas; and then, reproaching himself with charitable indulgence, he would toss off a review or an essay to make up the deficiency.

There was no doubt of his standing with the world. Cadell's new edition was going prodigiously; it was paying handsomely. He had thought that 1835 would see him clear of all debt, once more master of himself and his estates; now Cadell thought he could shorten that by two or even three years. After all his life insurance was twenty thousand pounds. If he did not live to clear off the rest of the debt that would do it. With luck he

would, however, see himself a debtless man; he would
be able to leave his insurance as well as his royalties to
his children. Already his books, his furniture, and his
curiosities were his to bequeath. His creditors had been
so pleased at the industry and popularity which had already paid them better than they could possibly have
expected, which gave every promise of shortly paying
them the full twenty shillings in the pound, that they
had handsomely released all claim to these things, asking him to accept them with their thanks and appreciation.

He might be old; he might be ill; winter weather
cursed him with chilblains on fingers and on toes —
almost he had said on mind — he had need of a staff to
walk by and the hand of an amanuensis to write by; but
he was not beaten yet; he would never be beaten. He
had once thought it impossible to clear off this weight of
debt; but he would not die like a poisoned rat in a hole;
he would not have it written on his monument that he
had not tried; he had rather die at his desk than be a
shirker. He had taken the long tedious path of duty
feeling that it led to "true fame and stainless reputation"; if he died in harness he would die with honor.
He would not be the sport of circumstances; he had
shown his ability to rise above misfortune; he had shown
himself able to ride with the oppressive harness; and now
the time was at hand when he would throw it off.

If some of these self-imposed tasks of literary labor
were such as his poverty not his will imposed, if he

had in the process become a creature such as he had often thought to despise, a hack writer, he must be forgiven because his task could not otherwise be finished in time. Besides he still had the will to help lesser writers. And there were the sons of other men to help; his own sons were already established, Charles in the Foreign Office, Walter a major in the army. When he had been in London he had had the satisfaction of getting from his political friends *two* cadetships for the sons of Allan Cunningham, who had not had influence enough to get *one*. He had helped various young men to commissions of various sorts. He had got a Chancery suit on the right train to yield something to his children on the claim of their mother. He had even been able to help his capable son-in-law. Lockhart was a clever man with an able pen; his judgment sometimes needed bolstering; this Parliamentary scheme of his would never do since he could not make a speech. There would be little use in his getting a seat if he could never make any real use of it. He never had been able to express himself on his feet; he was as stuttering and feeble in a speech as he was incisive and brilliant in print.

He was glad anyhow that he had not come to the point where no one sought his advice, where he was definitely shelved. He would not have liked that. He had been privately much amused with the uproar over his *Malachi* letters, he a man who had made a sad mess of his own finances telling the nation how to manage Great Britain's finances. He who had spilled the contents of his own purse upon the ground had actually attempted — and in great measure succeeded — in controlling the purse strings of the country.

At least he had not acted the part of a coward like James Ballantyne. James upon whom on the whole life had smiled (he would have been an obscure printer in Kelso had it not been for Sir Walter Scott), James had not been able to stand the gusts of adversity. At his wife's death he had retired abruptly to the country, leaving his business to get along or not, for all he seemed to care. He had moped and moped; he had turned to the strange fanaticisms of the chapel; he had talked religious nonsense instead of business. He had come back to town eventually when they had all protested against his ridiculous seclusion; but the pious cant hung round him still.

What would he have done if he had had to face the possibility of a duel ? poor spineless James — and yet one got tired of pitying him and began to dislike him heartily. Sir Walter Scott came near meeting his end in a duel; not that he would have minded much, though life had become placidly pleasant of late. General Gourgaud had chosen to take offence at the statements in the *Life of Napoleon*. The newspapers had had a jolly time of it. The old fool acted as if his rag of a reputation could be hurt. He, Sir Walter Scott, was not afraid of him or any Frenchman who had kissed Napoleon's breeches. If the crazy loon wanted a duel he'd find him ready enough. There was nothing in life any more to attach him to it so strongly that he need refuse a challenge.

He had once given up a trip to Wellington's camp while
hostilities were going on because he found Charlotte dis-
tressed in the extreme; the pleasure or profit to him
would, he then felt, not offset her anxiety. Now there
was no Charlotte to worry; he could take this fellow's
challenge. But he'd first have the fun of seeing him
squirm under fire of another sort; he would publish all
the correspondence on record; perhaps the general had
forgotten some of those letters he had so freely written ?
But the choleric general backed down after a few more
splutters; he had no desire to see those letters public
property.

It had been an amusing interlude, on the whole. It
had made him feel less old. He was, after all, getting
feeble. Walking was truly painful; he would not walk
at all except that he did not like to admit his feebleness;
and then he had no desire to die in his armchair. He
had a feeling that if he gave in to his lameness, his rheumatism, his headaches, he would go to pieces. The hours
in the courtroom were often boring but they lent a certain dignity to his life; they made an occupation which
demanded attention; they made him a part of the busy
world, not a useless onlooker. The drudgery he in-
flicted on himself he would dodge if he could; but it
was for his own advantage; indeed, for his own pleasure,
since his happiness depended upon his writing down the
cancellation of his obligations. He still managed to get
up at seven o'clock a good part of the time though now
and then he dawdled in bed until eight or nine. He still
worked hours a day though he often gave up much time

to company, and to exercise (he would not give up exercise yet, however painfully it racked his body); at Abbotsford there was once more the old parade of suppliants, actors with no part to play except that of beggar, poets with unpublished masterpieces, authors with a plethora of romance, ventriloquists whose art was as starved as their bodies and who were more grateful for the guinea and the plentiful meals than for the chance of displaying their talents to the company in the drawingroom.

Even in the darkest days immediately after the catastrophe he had not been able to refuse dispensing bounty; now he felt that his unusual success permitted him wider latitude.  He never had been able to say a good round no to a suppliant !  After all it was a pity if a man whose pen earned thirty thousand or so a year could not give a few guineas to those whose pen with difficulty earned shillings.

He was fortunate in that public favor had remained with him; it might so easily have turned from his novels and poems, spread before it in generous helpings by Cadell.  He was thankful that he had not counted too much on the public; he had valued it at its true worth. The public weighed good and bad qualities by the pound sterling. "Get a good name and you may write trash. Get a bad one and you may write like Homer without pleasing a single reader."  Fortunately for his creditors he had remained the spoiled child of success.  His head was not turned.  He knew well that if there was aught good in his prose or poetry it was the "hurried frankness of composition which pleases soldiers, sailors, and young people of bold and active disposition." He had been "no sigher in shades," no singer of fancies whistled on reeds. He had never framed immortal thoughts in immortal verse; when he wanted to express his own sentiments now he had to turn to Bobbie Burns or to Shakespeare. Some blockhead had written a poem comparing him to Shakespeare; all rot; he knew he wasn't fit to tie Shakespeare's shoe-laces.

He had been the singer and the writer of daring deeds; he had pleased himself in celebrating the bold Scotch heroes from whom he was descended. As a boy he had been fed with tales of the border chieftains, and he had loved best of all that intrepid ancestor who, finding his flocks woefully diminished, had leapt on horseback, ridden over the border, and returned with a goodly number of sheep "lifted" from some English gentleman's estate. His childhood had thriven on romance, being at first inactive. He could not remember the early fever which had robbed him of the use of his legs; he did remember vaguely how he used to lie by the fire in his grandfather's hall, with the wool of a newly slaughtered lamb about him. He remembered, too, how he had loved to lie on a sunny bank among the sheep, and how the herdsman had piped Scotch tunes to him. He had been a spoiled child, the darling of his grandparents and aunts and uncles. When he had finally gone back to his parents his mother had been amused at his precocity; she had shown him off to her friends. He remembered now how he had been constantly called upon to recite old ballads to admiring ladies.

He must be getting old, for his memory harked back to the days of his petted childhood. And now the memories of youth were crowding in. Lady Jane Stuart had sent for him recently, having found that they were neighbors in Edinburgh. She was very old now; and she took a mournful pleasure in weeping over bygone days. She reminded him of his courting of her daughter, pretty young Williamina, dead these many years. She had not known then how famous and rich he would become; no, he reminded himself savagely, nor had she known he would be held up before the world as the man who owed a hundred and twenty thousand pounds and had to write his fingers off to pay them. She had not dwelt on this though; she had dwelt upon his fame, his success; and she had delved in her memory for the doings of other days, when he had been a sentimental young man dancing to the tunes of her daughter's playing. He did not like to remember those days. He had been young and full of hope; he had been unbelievably credulous. The ending of that idyll of young love had scarred his heart. A young man's faith had been ruined. Lady Jane would not have made a bad bargain if she had given him her daughter's hand. He hoped that Willie (the old nickname slipped out naturally) had been happy. He knew that she had lived quietly and for the most part withdrawn from the world; he wondered how her gay nature had liked that. She had taken her title ready made; he had won his and bestowed it upon *his* wife. She would have enjoyed his triumphs; she would have had hours of glory her baronet had not given her. She had chosen security and present wealth; she had not chosen to share his budding career.

It was painful to him to reopen the old wounds, remember the old emotions. Lady Jane was very old; she enjoyed shedding tears over him. She told him again and again how she had followed his career with joy; how his own mother could not have triumphed more at his successes than she. At the time, however, she had not believed in him; neither had her daughter. But his Charlotte had. She had said from the beginning that he would be a great rich man.

That he had become in time for her to enjoy his reputation and his wealth. Poor Charlotte ! if she had only lived she would once again see him a great rich man. A year or two more, granted his health and his continued popularity, and he would stand a free man, a rich man. He would not let up on this drudgery of writing, writing, even though he now knew that without further effort everything would be cleared: there was his insurance, and there were the large royalties from the works in print. He would continue working that he might during his life enjoy the complete repose that would come with all his bills discharged.

He would have more time for writing from now on. The court was to lessen the number of clerks; as he was the oldest it was therefore incumbent upon him to retire. If he retired his stipend would fall considerably short of the thirteen hundred pounds a year he now drew as salary; it would, he found, be exactly eight hundred and forty pounds a year. He would easily make up the difference by writing.

He was somewhat pained when he was offered a pension of five hundred a year to make up the discrepancy. This savored of charity. He was no disabled pensioner; he had his faculties; he could earn enough. Perhaps, though, his creditors would feel that he had no call to be high and mighty; perhaps they might reproach him if he followed his pride and refused the offer. He would, he supposed, have to consult them. He put the case before his trustees. Here were five hundred pounds a year to be his for the mere pocketing of his pride; he hoped, however, that the trustees would feel that he was warranted in refusing this offer; he was sure that they would not suffer from his refusal, as he would write the harder to make up that sum and more. He was pleased when he received their answer that his honorable efforts, and his immense success made it unnecessary for him to accept anything which seemed to him inconsistent with his pride. They were satisfied to rely upon his unaided efforts to discharge their claims.

So he would go to Abbotsford foot free. He would be glad not to have to toil to and from court, to live in lodgings where his rooms were furnished with the things he and Charlotte had chosen with such pride for 39 Castle Street; furnishings bought by friends or strangers, to decorate rooms foreign to him. He would be glad to be settled permanently in the country. Yet solitude was

not a good thing. It led to a vitiating of one's powers. He must not become a hermit; he must cultivate
society.

It was curious how he missed an occupation that had
seemed wearisome. He had often lamented the waste of
time listening to dull cases and poring over dull papers.
He had of late found difficulty and weariness walking
to and from court. He ought to be glad to be relieved
of the necessity. And yet he was not glad.

Since there was no longer any necessity for him to
go about he found himself more unwilling to make the
effort to stir from his desk. He had taken to working in
the library; his study was too hot in fine weather. His
handwriting left much to be desired these days. What
would his sons and his nephew say to it now ? he had
so constantly reproached them with their chicken tracks
and upheld the virtues of a clear, neat hand. His words
trailed across the paper; he could not always make them
out himself. He was getting old.

He was not alarmed over the writing; he could always
hire an amanuensis. He was alarmed over his unruly
tongue which had taken to betraying him. It would not
utter the words he thought to say; sometimes it would
utter nothing at all. It was disconcerting, to say the
least, to be halted in mid speech. He tried not to show
Anne how alarmed he was when this happened. He had
for years now feared palsy and paralysis. His parents
had been prey to paralysis, his brothers. He passionately
protested against a fate that would deprive him of speech

and of locomotion, leaving him a powerless hulk, a dumb lion to be stared at. He did not want to die while life held anything for him. He did not want to live on after mental death.

But his health mended after generous cuppings and bleedings; he would like to think that his last attack had been due to his stomach; he would like to put his suspicions to sleep. Meanwhile he could get about on a quiet pony which was exercise enough for an old fellow of sixty. He had lost all foolish pride; he could take his daily pony ride with servants before and behind him; it took two of them to lift him to the poor beast's back; and they accompanied him lest he take a tumble and break his brittle old bones. It was kind of them to care. His servants had not deserted him when the crash came; they had remained to work the harder in his service and take upon themselves outdoor tasks as well.

Still the house was lonely; he was glad to have a brace of visitors arrive even though they did interrupt his steady work. He made a few visits, took to dining out with his neighbors. Old friends came to Abbotsford bringing their grown sons with them. And then, with a house full of guests, he was once more struck down with paralysis.

It was only a slight attack which came to him in his room. Anne had sent word to the guests to breakfast without them; but he had been able to get down for dinner. It was foolish of Anne to be alarmed, to send the guests off next day when he was already recovered. He had thought for a few hours that his end had come;

but he had pulled himself together; and now he was himself once more.

He never knew that he had come to table with his guests, the pale ghost of even his aged self. He had tottered to a chair and looked about in a confused way. Food he had refused. Then he had begun in a quavering voice one of his favorite anecdotes. As he told of the pauper lunatic who, imagining himself to be playing host to great personages at a fine banquet, complained to the doctor that all the grand food tasted to him like oatmeal porridge, Sir Walter's voice gained in firmness. It remained low but it did not falter. The guests had begun to eat, greatly relieved. Their host's humor brought laughter. Anne's anxious countenance became less drawn, more cheerful. A few minutes later Sir Walter began again to speak. Quite pleasantly he retold the anecdote. There was polite laughter at its close. Anne's face took on a worried expression. A few moments later Sir Walter began the story again and went through it without pause. At Anne's gesture the guests rose, as if the meal were ended. Sir Walter, leaning on his daughter's arm, retired to his own room. The next day Abbotsford was empty of guests save for two sober physicians who had hurried from town to give succor and advice.

May weather and the arrival of the Lockharts with two healthy youngsters and the invalid Johnie helped to divert Sir Walter's thoughts. He was conscious of impaired speech, yet on the whole confident. He feared palsy, he dreaded a return of illness that would confine him to his chair. Yet with characteristic optimism he decided that even such a life might be tolerable; one's desires would contract with one's capacities. One's circle necessarily narrowed as one grew older. His physical circle was already cramped; so far he thought his mental circle had not ceased to widen. He would not like to give up physical activity, he who had in the past been unusually vigorous. Still, even if he filled the mortal span of threescore and ten, he would not have to suffer many years. So long as his mental strength held he would not pine. Sometimes he feared that his mind was giving way; he doubted if he wrote with the old power and fire. Ballantyne croaked that he didn't, but then all Ballantyne would have him write would be chivalry and tournaments. And Ballantyne had not shown himself so strong of mind in facing his own actions. He could not write just to please James.

It was pleasant to be relieved of gloomy forebodings by visitors. Wordsworth, friendly as ever, came for three days and was shown the neighborhood. Everyone combined to advise Scott to try a change of climate before the winter. He would suffer cruelly from the cold in Scotland; why should he not do as he was urged and spend the cold months in a milder clime? The King had put a frigate at his disposal; his children, all but Sophia who must stay with her babies, were eager to go with him. He was, though he hated to confess even to himself, perturbed over his increasing bodily weaknesses, his intermittent cloudiness of mind. He would go travelling and seek a cure in change of scene.

The Mediterranean trip offered much diversion, new

scenes of romance, new friends. Foreign booksellers offered the travellers pictures of British scenes, first and
foremost views of Abbotsford. But the great man was
rapidly failing; his mind he felt to be clearer than ever
as he gathered data for future literary labors; his body was
fast becoming immovable. He declined an audience with
the Pope; he had to forego many a pleasant excursion; it
was too difficult to walk, too impossible to climb stairs.
It was a satisfaction to dwell not on present disabilities
but upon the accomplishments of a lifetime; whatever
satisfaction he had from his rising from an obscure young
lawyer to the greatest literary figure of his generation,
from an impecunious sheriff to a landed baronet, was
obscured by his greatest triumph, that of successfully
undertaking the discharge of mountainous debts. He
had faced a deficit of one hundred and twenty thousand
pounds; he would, he thought, be clear of the whole
amount by midsummer. He would stand a free man.
The prodigious sale of his poems and novels would divert
to his own pocket once more the handsome royalties.
He would yet buy that estate to add to his holdings.

Sometimes he fancied that the debt was already discharged; then he would remember. He would have to
work hard just a little longer. But there was no longer
room for doubt of his complete success; even if he wrote
no more, even if he died, his affairs were in such order
that the royalties would make all clear.

He began to long for Abbotsford. These foreign views
were very fine, these new friends were very attentive;
he longed for a sight of the Tweed, of the woods his own

hand had planned and planted, of the familiar Scotch faces. The journey home would be long and, he feared, tedious. He yielded to his children's desire that he should make it in the greatest possible comfort. He bought a carriage for two hundred pounds, a spacious, well-hung vehicle which could, if need be, accommodate him with the comfort of a bed. He was eager to get home. Yet he paused in Rome, in any place where Anne wished to sight-see. He took no pleasure in new sights himself; he would not, however, curtail her enjoyment. But his working days were not many now; he must get to Abbotsford and write at his own desk. Even if the debts were safely provided for he must write; the habit of years was not to be broken.

Reaching London he was too ill to be moved farther. For a month he lay, bled and cupped and blistered. There was apparently only one invalid in all London. When people met on the street, at restaurants, at the theatre, the first question was "Do you know how Sir Walter is ?" The street where he lay was thronged with inquirers. The royal family sent daily for bulletins.

The invalid was patient. His desire to go home to Abbotsford did not lessen as the month wore on. Finally he started on the last lap of the journey. He reached Edinburgh safely. Then began the drive out to Abbotsford. As familiar sights came into view, as the Tweed unrolled itself before his eye the invalid brightened. It was happiness to be once more under his own roof, the magnificent roof he had fashioned from his own labors. This was his monument, this the testimony to his work.

SIR WALTER SCOTT
*From a painting by Sir Thomas Lawrence*

He had wrought this out of his own fancy. No inherited wealth his; no ancestral hall. He had built the hall for his descendants, he had surrounded it with fair acres. The woods of his planting would last long.

He was impatient to visit his domain. He was too weak to walk; he could no longer bestride a pony. In an invalid's chair he made the tour of his gardens; in an invalid's chair he made the tour of his halls. This was a bonnier sight than Italian marble. Day after day he made his tours of inspection. Then he reproached himself for temporising. He would get to work once more. He had himself wheeled to his desk; he bade friends and servants leave him there to write. But the pen fell from the poor stiff fingers. Illness had conquered him; he would struggle no more; he would go to bed.

The days went dreamily by. He was conscious of the presence of all his loved ones, all but little Johnie Lockhart whose brief span had closed. They tried, these children of his, to make him comfortable. It was not hard to die thus, his life's work ended. He had started life an invalid — at least he had become one at the early age of eighteen months. He had been the centre of a household for many years, waited upon, coaxed, coddled. He had come full circle it would seem.

His mind often wandered. He lived again the scenes of his childhood, fought again the battles of boyhood. Lame, he had never been able to fight like other boys; but his schoolfellows had met him on his own ground; many a bloody battle had he enjoyed, he and his opponent sitting opposite each other on a school bench and hammering at each other with right good will.

His life had been full; he had had adventure, success, riches, fame. He had in six years cleared off debts that would have resisted the efforts of many a man's lifetime. On the whole he was content. There was nothing in his life, nothing in all his books, that could have hurt any man. He had lived a clean life; he had written clean books. He had been healthy of mind and of body.

He called his son-in-law to his bedside, trying to sum up for him his own philosophy: "Lockhart, I may have but a minute to speak to you. My dear, be a good man — be virtuous — be religious — be a good man. Nothing else will give you any comfort when you come to lie here."

And thus he died, this apostle of strength, of firm purpose, of boyish fun and manly achievement. He had been hard riding squire, mercenary land-buyer, and the greatest literary figure of the early nineteenth century. No poet with head in the clouds was he; no romancer indifferent to the world's rewards. A plain man, an honest man, he wrote as he lived with a healthy vigor beside which genius seemed to have a sickly hue.

In death as in life he was accorded the honors of royalty. He died as he had lived, great rich man.

# IMPORTANT DATES
# IN WALTER SCOTT'S LIFE

Born, Edinburgh, August 15, 1771
Admitted to the bar, 1792
Married Charlotte Carpenter, December 24, 1797
Abbotsford, 1814
Baronetcy 1820
Financial Catastrophe 1826
Died, September 21, 1832

*Important Publications*

1802 Border Minstrelsy
1805 Lay of the Last Minstrel
1808 Marmion
1808 Edition of Dryden
1810 The Lady of the Lake
1814 Edition of Swift
     Waverley
1815 Guy Mannering
1816 The Antiquary
     The Black Dwarf
     Old Mortality
1818 Rob Roy
     The Heart of Midlothian
1819 The Bride of Lammermoor
     A Legend of Montrose
1820 Ivanhoe
     The Monastery
     The Abbot
1821 Kenilworth
1822 The Pirate
     The Fortunes of Nigel

1823 Peveril of the Peak
       Quentin Durward
1824 St. Ronan's Well
       Redgauntlet
1825 The Betrothed
       The Talisman
1826 Woodstock
1827 The Two Drovers
       The Highland Widow
       The Surgeon's Daughter
       Life of Napoleon
1828 The Fair Maid of Perth
1829 Anne of Geierstein
1831 Count Robert of Paris
       Castle Dangerous